SERIOUSLY SOCIAL

TURNING YOUR ONLINE GAME
INTO REAL-WORLD GAIN

By

SIMONE DOUGLAS

Cover design: Lucy Rose
Typesetting: Clockwork Graphic Design
Printing: Printed in Australia by Ovato Print Pty Ltd

Published by Peritia Press

Contents

Foreword

First impressions are really important. This is something that BNI members implicitly understand, because it is central to everything we do but even more than this, the impressions you make ongoing are equally critical.

The split second judgements people make are formed in a myriad of ways, but many key factors we rely on to convey information about ourselves, such as body language and tone of voice, are lost in the digital realm. The way that business is conducted these days means that you will often meet someone in a digital environment long before you meet them face-to-face. So it is crucial that your online presence is truly representative of who you are and what you do.

Where *Seriously Social* brings real value is through

calling upon you to consider the long-term game plan for your digital footprint, from a personal brand-building perspective, from the very beginning of contact. When you get this brand-building right, it has the capacity to support you in achieving your business goals and your personal dreams. More than that, though, it also supports your wider network in solving their problems and achieving their goals. *And this is the new model for doing business.*

The reality is that the pre-digital, transactional 'burn and turn' model for doing business, where people are constantly looking for the next person and then the next person, is no longer effective. Inevitably, there comes a point when they run out of networks to burn.

The new model enables people to build the network of a lifetime. As I say in my book *Who's In Your Room?*, be very careful about who you open the door to. But it could be equally said, be really cognizant of who it is that you're inviting to the party. Whether or not you open the door is the next step. Who you give out your "address" to is really the blueprint for building your optimum network.

The way in which Simone has built her network, both online and through BNI, is a great example of how this works. Although her company, Social Media AOK, had only been operating for three months when Simone joined BNI in 2012, the 'givers gain' ethos of BNI resonated perfectly with her own understanding of what it means to be in business. Rather than focusing on what other people could do for her, she recognised that what she was able to offer other people held the key to developing successful relationships. Known in her networks these days as "the Oracle", she has cemented herself as the key person of influence able to solve challenges for those connected to her seamlessly and in a way that is always lifting people up to the next level - a true reflection of living Givers Gain.

Through developing those relationships, Simone quickly became part of the BNI Australia team, working closely with Frederick Marcoux, National Director of BNI Australia, to build a really effective social media presence for numerous BNI members in a way that supports their chapters and their businesses.

Once Simone had become a member of the BNI Australia team, I connected with her at a BNI global convention, through the one-to-one time that I spend with each team from around the globe. Simone was one of our presenters at the 2019 BNI global convention in Poland. Her topic, "Seriously Social - the BNI Playbook", was well received as a practical and no-nonsense approach to building your brand for real world gain.

My knowledge of Simone through the BNI global conventions, combined with her close working relationship with Australia's National Director Frederick Marcoux, meant that when Simone thought of me to write the foreword for *Seriously Social*, I was happy to oblige.

Networking is not only about building key relationships, it's also about understanding the interconnectedness of those relationships. This is exactly in line with my keynote about 'networking up'. Because once you've put the money in the favour bank, you have the opportunity to cash in when you really need to.

Simone's personal brand-building, online and

face-to-face, is a case in point when it comes to how to achieve your goals through networking. Having helped numerous businesses create their own successful digital footprints, Simone is now sharing her strategies and insights on a larger scale. I can highly recommend *Seriously Social* as a great resource for anyone looking to create and leverage their digital network to grow their business in a truly remarkable and sustainable way.

Dr. Ivan Misne
New York Times Bestselling Author and Founder of BNI

Chapter One

Mistaking The Tool For The Solution

So often, people come to social media expecting money to rain from the sky. This happens because there is a belief that going digital is a silver bullet for marketing and that, just by jumping onto various platforms, all their problems will be solved.

Although it is true that social media can be a really fast and effective route to market, the reality is that *it is just like any other tool*. And as with any tool, whether it is a piece of software or a hammer, if you don't know how to use it then you're going to make a dog's breakfast of whatever you try to do.

The Purpose, The Aim, And The Art Of Being Seen

Suppose that an enthusiastic business owner creates a shiny new Facebook page and LinkedIn account. They feel very pleased with their work, and sit back to wait for the money to start raining down.

Unfortunately, they quickly become very confused and distressed, because the buckets they put out to catch all the magical sky dollars aren't filling up. *So where did they go wrong?* Quite simply, they haven't understood the purpose of being on these platforms.

The purpose of social media is to create an opportunity for people to get to know you.

The aim is to develop things to the point where people like you, trust you, and have some sort of relationship with your brand or your business. All of which is straightforward enough, but how do you achieve it?

Firstly, you need to make a time commitment. This means turning up on those platforms regularly. However, just being online isn't enough. You need your presence to reflect who you are and what you're about. The most important element of this is that **you need to be prepared to be seen.**

So many businesses fill their platforms with a very carefully crafted marketing message. The problem is that it has nothing to do with who they are as a business. Social media can be extremely effective if you're prepared to be real, authentic, and transparent. However, it can take courage to do this.

Example - Home Alone

Let's imagine there's an Australian mortgage broker who wants to sell more home loans. The cover photo on his Facebook page is a lovely stock image of an American dream home.

The house looks great, but the architecture is very different from the properties that his potential customers are familiar with, and so it automatically creates a subconscious sense that something is not quite right.

His feed reinforces this feeling. It is full of carefully branded glossy photos and company logos. The images are attractive, but instantly forgettable. People tend to just glance over them and move on.

He's not connecting with his audience, and so he is unable to increase the number of loans he is selling.

Many marketers will tell you that organic reach is dead on Facebook. They will tell you that Facebook now fits into a 'pay to play' model, and that you have to put money behind it to push your content. I'm happy to let you know that this this simply isn't true!

Case Study - Small Change

When it comes to marketing, it is easy to get really caught up in strategy. All businesses who have a social media strategy will talk about how many followers they want to have, their levels of engagement, how much traffic they will drive to the website, and how many conversions they will have at the end of it all. They work out the figures and then they set the budget.

Of course there is a place for this, but they are missing a trick. If you have a *narrative strategy*, with a clear idea of the story that you are telling about your business, then your content is always going to be much more powerful. This is all about organic reach.

Taking my pub as an example, The Duke of Brunswick is the Seriously Social pub on Gilbert Street. *What does that mean?* It means that we solve our customers' problems so that they can be seriously social too.

One of the ways we achieve this is by having a gluten-free kitchen. This ensures that anyone who is a coeliac can eat at the pub and have a great, stress-free meal with their dining companions.

Once we switched the kitchen to gluten-free, I noticed that we were attracting more and more families, which was a new thing for us. Families bring babies, and so we needed to provide changing facilities. There was room for a change table in both the men's and the women's toilets, and so it seemed logical to provide facilities to change the babies in both.

The narrative was that we were solving a problem for our customers. The content was very simple. It was just a photo of two change tables, with a man and a woman standing behind them, and it said, '*With so many families coming in we thought we had best get a change table but we didn't want to discriminate so we got two! There are now change tables in both the men's and women's toilets because dads need access to change tables too.*'

70,000 people liked that post within twelve hours. It was shared hundreds of times all over the country. Although it was about us solving a problem for our clients, it was also a topic that people felt really strongly about.

It's an issue for dads that they often don't have anywhere to change their babies. So we hit all of those emotional tones and created a space in that content where the people who were impacted by this problem felt seen and heard. It was through this that we got great traction.

The photo wasn't glossy or styled; it was just a snapshot of something that happened in the pub that day. In fact, I have posted some pretty poor quality images on the Duke of Brunswick's social media platforms, and a number of those images have gone viral - for all the right reasons.

Having the right content, being prepared to be yourself, and trusting that this is ok is a really powerful way to get the most out of your social media.

Vacant Or Engaged?

One way to ensure you are creating the right content is to **ask questions that you genuinely want answers to.** In this respect, social media is no different to interacting with people face-to-face. *You need to find ways to start conversations, and asking questions is a great way to do that.*

I will often have clients scroll back through their content to find examples of questions that weren't rhetorical. A lot of the time months and months will have gone by without a question being posted that actually required an answer. And yet they still wonder why there is no engagement.

In many cases, it simply hasn't occurred to them to actively engage with their audience. This is easily fixed, as all that is required is an awareness that it needs to be done.

On the other hand, there are a number of people who are concerned about posting a question that no one answers, and just being left to watch the digital tumbleweed roll by. This is a practical problem, and as with all practical problems there is a practical solution. **Bait the hook!**

If you are worried that people won't comment on your post, then contact your friends and family. Let them know that you're going to be posting a question, and ask them to help you out by volunteering their opinions. This can be particularly helpful on Facebook, as the platform will see it as solid peer-to-peer engagement, which then pushes your content further in the news feed.

Start With The End In Mind

If you know which social media platforms you want to be on, what you want those platforms to do for you, and which aspects of your business you want them to represent, then you give yourself purpose and direction.

We increasingly look to brands for transparency, and so part of what you want your platforms to do for you is demonstrate to your stakeholders and customers what the values and ethics of your business are.

The best place to start is to **ask yourself who you are as a business.** When a customer walks into your store or your office, or picks up the phone to call you, what is it that you want them to feel? And what are the behaviours that you and your staff engage in to demonstrate those values?

By answering these questions you will have a clear idea of what you need to be talking about on social media.

The bottom line is that if you are not putting up content that is telling your story and supporting your values then you are unlikely to gain many followers or make many connections. This problem is reinforced by a lack of engagement, as your content won't get pushed, and not many people will see what you are posting.

Mind The Gap

Taking the time to develop a narrative strategy and give your social media accounts a bit of a massage is central to being seen by the right people.

To give you an example, your personal LinkedIn account is one of the most important tools that you have at your disposal in business. Yet so many people just throw up a photo and a headline, with a bit of a 'look at me' summary. Then they wonder why they don't make any friends.

LinkedIn is effectively your online dating profile for business, and so how you present yourself is really important.

Going back to pre-history, when people put personal ads in the paper, if your ad stated that you enjoyed long walks on the beach and playing chess by the fire, but when you turn up for your date it quickly transpires that you like motor sports and cans of beer, then you will quickly disappear into the gap between the fiction and the fact.

The point of presenting yourself in the best possible light is not to stretch the truth until it is unrecognisable. The point is to make a good impression. This is so important, because the reality is that the first online opinion of your personal brand is really powerful.

This means that **what people see when they look at your LinkedIn account needs to be a true representation of who you are.** You can choose where you shine the spotlight, but it will always come back to the same thing.

You need to be genuine and authentic, and let people see what matters to you. By doing this, you can connect with the people who truly want to form a relationship with your brand. Otherwise you're wasting everyone's time.

For some business owners, letting people have these insights can feel daunting. We are taught from a young age to hide ourselves, and the older you get the more ingrained that behaviour becomes.

When you combine this with a fear of the unknown, which arises when people don't have a concept or an understanding of what they're doing or where they're going, taking that leap of faith and letting people see who you are can seem quite difficult.

The truth is that you can't please all of the people all of the time. And so you need to focus on the ones who matter. The thought to keep in mind is that every time you post something online, whether it is on a personal account or a business account, you are either opening an opportunity or closing an opportunity.

Example - Keep It Constant And Selective

I am friends with lots of people on Facebook who I spend time with socially. I am also friends with lots of people who I have met at conferences and events. As a result, I am aware that anything I post needs to embrace both these groups of people.

In order to present an image that is both personal and professional, a lot of my content is about the travelling and teaching that I do for work. My kids are not part of my marketing strategy, but if I do post a photo of them I am aware that alongside the intended audience, which is my friends and family, there will be people I know professionally who will see these pictures.

This is not a negative. It allows me to be a bit more human in their eyes, by showing that I am more than just a businesswoman - I am also a busy single mum.

People don't like to analyse their lives in this

way, but the inescapable fact is that every single time you post anything online you are adding another piece of information to the narrative you are creating. The same is true for everyone.

Every Single One's Got A Story To Tell

All of your business connections, every friend, and each member of your family are telling their own stories. They are all presenting an image that they want the world to see, whether it is the beautiful meal they created, the incredible mountain they snowboarded down, or the amazing contract they secured.

They will post the content that reinforces the image they want to present - even if they spent the morning curled up in the foetal position crying on the floor.

In fact, for someone like Agony Autie, who is raising awareness of living with autism, part of the focus may be on the times when they *are* curled up crying. Who you are online doesn't necessarily have to be shiny and happy, but it does need to be truthful and help people connect with what you are saying.

Even when you understand why it is important to present a truthful picture, the idea of laying your life open to the world can still seem a bit overwhelming. And the more open you are, the more vulnerable you can feel. *So where do you find the confidence to let people see who you are and what you care about?*

Exercise - The Thirty-Day Challenge

One way to build your confidence is to take part in a thirty-day challenge. These are challenges based around doing one thing every day for thirty days in a row.

A popular one is the thirty-day video challenge, where you film yourself and upload the video to your social media platforms every day for a month. If you're uncomfortable posting anything, then this probably feels like throwing yourself into the shark-infested deep end.

A less intense alternative would be to challenge yourself to do *something* on your

---

> social media channels every day for thirty days. This could be as straightforward as sharing an article – but if this is the route you take then you still need to include *why* you are sharing that article, by outlining the reasons you think it matters.

There is too much white noise in the social media space, and one of the biggest problems is that everyone is contributing to this noise, instead of contributing value.

This is where you can learn from the mistakes of others. Don't be that person you meet at a party who just talks about themselves non-stop. People can't get away from that person quickly enough!

Equally, you don't want to be the shrinking violet in the corner, who is desperately hoping someone will come and talk to them. You need to find the middle ground.

Ultimately, the aim is the same as all marketing - you need to make it about your audience, rather than about yourself.

Batteries Are Not Included!

As we have established, when it comes to social media the batteries are not included. You can't just sit back and expect everything to take care of itself. You really do have to keep feeding the platforms with content.

We have also seen that you can't just chuck any old rubbish into the machine. *You need to have conversations with people about things they are actually interested in.*

Where a lot of businesses go wrong when they are trying to achieve this is that they don't know what their personality is. They spend so much time doing buyer personas and studies into key market segments, but when it comes to knowing what their tone of voice is, they haven't really thought about it.

Exercise – Who Are You?

A really fun exercise to uncover your tone of voice is to ask yourself one question. *If your brand was a famous person, who would it be?* Generally speaking, as a team, you can clarify

> what the attributes of a business are. You can
> then line this up with the public persona of
> a famous person. The minute you know that
> you're Oprah Winfrey or Hugh Jackman, you
> can ask if what you are doing is in line with that
> personality.

What Would Hugh Do?

When you look at every piece of content and ask if it
fits with your brand persona, you will quickly come
to see whether or not it aligns. You may decide that
an image is too flat. You may notice that the sentence
structure doesn't seem quite right. You may realise
that the entire post isn't exciting enough. In every
single case you have a clear touch point you can refer
to in order to ensure you stay on message. *This should
apply on and offline.*

If someone walks through the door of your
business, and that business is Hugh Jackman, is
that who they will meet? Or are they going to find
themselves face-to-face with Neil from The Young
Ones?

It's all very well having a great online persona, but if it has nothing to do with who your customers speak to on the phone or see in your office or store, then it is meaningless.

Developing a brand persona is a really good way of identifying other problems in the business. Ultimately, it doesn't matter what your brand is - if it's not intrinsically the culture within your business then you have far bigger issues than marketing.

So developing your brand persona has implications that reach far beyond social media, and can provide you with an opportunity to see if there are issues that need addressing.

It is also a really easy way to let your staff know what you are going for. By asking them to think about *how* they are 'Hugh Jackman' in their day-to-day work you can take them closer to what it is you need from them.

Find out the five ways they are 'Hugh Jackman' every day. It could be that they always answer the phone with a smile on their face. It could be that they are extremely loyal and trustworthy.

When you have developed your brand persona, the only question your staff need to ask themselves is, 'What would that person do?'

What Does It Look Like When Everything Is Aligned?

Going back to the Duke of Brunswick, 90% of the posts that I put up for the pub have people in them. This ensures our customers feel invested in the pub, because they feel as though they know the staff.

Every time we have an announcement about a public holiday, there will be a picture of Eden holding the bookings book. If we are letting people know that our gluten-free beer is going on tap, we post a photo of Courtney and Jen standing on the bar, pointing at the tap.

We let our customers know that we are excited about the things that have meaning in their lives. We will post pictures of chef Dave and chef Adam at the end of a busy shift to let our customers know that, even though they are exhausted, they still love you. There is a sense of humour and a lot of fun in what we do.

We also ensure that we don't leave comments to chance. There are a variety of monitoring tools you can use, such as Hootsuite and Agora Pulse, which are my two favourites, but as the business owner I have Pages Manager on my phone, and I check it two or three times a day.

This is because you can't really replace that authentic first person voice with an agency. Having said that, you can get close. This is when your brand persona becomes crucial, because the agency needs to know what they are meant to sound like when they respond to posts.

Example – Skin Deep Content

Skincare offers many examples of how not to do social media. One famous Australian skincare brand posts nothing but shots of their products and their raw ingredients, or yet another competition. Other than this, there is really not much content.

This is such a shame, because the company has an amazing backstory, fantastic staff, and, due to their wide appeal, the opportunity to use their customers as brand ambassadors.

They could have taken an extremely humanistic approach to spreading the brand. Instead, they defaulted to 'here's another photo of our moisturiser' and 'here's another photo of our face mask'. The problem is that no one is going to engage with that.

Larger companies are frequently the ones who get it wrong. This is because what people crave is that raw, authentic content and those 'behind the scenes' stories.

A great way for larger companies to address this is through user-generated content and user experiences, which are really powerful ways to reach your audience.

Example – Social Insects

Although it is easy to get social media wrong, it isn't difficult to get it right. Burt's Bees is a great example of how a skincare company has achieved a really solid narrative.

It's all about the bees. Their whole thing is 'Bring Back The Bees' and 'Make A Difference', so their customers are able to feel really good about buying their products.

This is not only because people feel good about supporting a company whose values they share, and which also happens to make great products. It is also because they know that when the purchase Burt's Bees products they are doing something bigger that has a positive impact on the bee population and, by extension, the entire ecosystem.

It translates as, 'Buy a lovely lip balm and help save the planet!' and 'For just a few dollars, you can have soft skin and feel like a superhero!' That's a powerful message to send out!

Key Takeaways

- When you understand that the tool is not the solution, it is simply a tool, you can start exploring how to use it effectively.

- Make sure you show up on all your platforms regularly – you need to be seen and stay front-of-mind

- Be authentically you! This will happen naturally when you understand your brand persona, share your values, and keep it constant.

Chapter Two

Plan To Plan Or Plan To Fail

So, you're on social media. You've picked your platforms, based on recommendations from colleagues, friends, and family. You've been posting pretty pictures of things you believe are representative of who you are as a company, and yet they have no alignment with what you are trying to achieve in your business.

When we look at why this happens, the first point to address is the way in which social media marketing is viewed by many businesses. It's kind of like a younger sibling – it can be fun to play with or it can be extremely annoying, but beyond that it's just sort of *there*. As a result, social media is often not integrated into the main marketing and communications plan.

I believe that sales and marketing are increasingly one function, which means that any marketing and communications strategy needs to be aligned with your top-line goals for the business.

This means that if you are using social media marketing, you can't just shove it to one side and ignore it. **Your strategy needs to incorporate all aspects of marketing.**

But how do you align your social media strategy with your top-line goals?

Example - Highlighting The Benefits

Let's say you are a local hairdresser and you would like to bring in an extra $2,000.00 a month. Based on what I pay my hairdresser, this seems like a realistic goal! For a high-end salon this would roughly equate to an extra seven clients having a full head of foils each month.

What do these clients look like who will happily sit down and pay $300.00 to have their hair done? For argument's sake, let's say they live within five kilometres of the salon, they are generally over the age of forty, they have an interest in good quality fashion labels, they tend to be business owners or management-level professionals, and they may well be divorced.

When you package this up you have a group of women who are probably very conscious of their appearance. You can see how we are starting to align the top-line business goal of bringing in an extra $2,000.00 a month with a profile of our ideal customer.

Once we have a clear idea who we are speaking to, then it becomes about what they are actually interested in. What are the pain points for these ideal clients? What is the problem we are solving for them?

If you can post things that show these women how their hair can be easier to manage, how they can style it quickly and still look fantastic, or how they can extend the time between visits to the salon, then you are very likely to catch their attention.

However, you don't need to limit yourself to

what *you* can offer them. For example, as these women are very aware of their appearance there is a good chance they will have an interest in skincare.

So if you go down the street and talk to the local beautician and ask them to come and do a Facebook live video talking about how to do a five-minute skincare routine that will save time and leave skin glowing, then you will achieve a number of objectives.

Firstly, you have made a new referral partner, because you are giving exposure to a non-competitive business that's aligned with what you do. You also get yourself in front of their customers, because they will share the video to their channels.

Not only this, but you have provided real value for your existing clients, *and* you have started a conversation with people who don't know your business. Being able to achieve all of these things is something worth putting money behind.

When you are creating a marketing strategy, you should have both short-term goals and long-term goals – **and these goals should be aligned with the business.**

All too often a decision is made that the company needs to post five times a week, and that the posts will be about what is happening in the business.

The problem with this is that there is no real thought put into who your business needs to talk to more, what you need to talk to them about, how it is going to benefit the business, and what the path to growing your market is. Generally speaking, your strategy should be that coherent.

Once you have your business goals, and you know who you want to talk to, you can work out how to find them, and what you need to post that is going to engage them.

Going back to the example of the hairdresser, it is a little like dropping a pebble into a pond. The ripples quickly spread. This means that if you can get the interest and attention of one woman who wants a full head of foils, then you are likely to attract her friends, and so on.

Seasons and Cycles

Once you have established who you want to talk to and how to reach them, the next element that you need to put in place is a **twelve-week content cycle.**

*You should be planning four weeks in advance for the coming four weeks' content. Once that four weeks of content has rolled out you should spend some time over the following four weeks evaluating what worked, what didn't work, what you could have done better, and which bits are now **evergreen content** that can be used again the following year.*

Evergreen content is great to have. This is because, generally speaking, the same things happen in your business every year. So, if you are a business-to-business (B2B) company then you will have the same peaks and troughs every year.

You can pretty much map them. This enables you to build out from your twelve-week content cycle to give you a picture of what will be happening over a twelve-month period.

You know that the danger periods in a B2B environment are December and January, because clients will often cancel their contracts over this period, as they have the time to reconsider their needs while they are on holiday. Likewise, May to June can be tricky, as we come into budget-time and businesses start evaluating their spending.

If your company is business-to-consumer then you have a whole calendar of holidays and events that dictate your retail trends, but you will also have a lot of other seasonal considerations that impact on your business, which may be related to your product range, location, or any number of other factors.

Exercise - Planning To Plan

If you map out all of these events on a calendar then you can proactively push sales of a specific product or service six weeks out from a particular event, to help bullet-proof the business or smooth out the peaks and troughs.

Once you have this map, you can begin to plan your content. For example, you can consider your themes and your focus for the month of March. You can decide what you are going to take advantage of, and what specials or promotions you want to offer.

You can also work out the people you need to make friends with, and who already has those people as an audience. Once you have a clear idea of this then you will know where you want to be seen. It's a bit like being at high school - you want to make sure you're with all the 'cool kids'.

Once you have outlined everything then it becomes a rolling mechanism, but it *is* something that you have to set aside time in you diary to do. The reality is, **if you don't set aside time in your diary for the entire year then you are failing to plan – and therefore, planning to fail.**

When you are setting time aside you might decide that your content planning will take place during the second week of the month, and that you're going to spend four hours on it. Alternatively, you may decide to spend one hour a week on it. **No matter how you choose**

> to allocate your content planning time, you
> have to be religious with it.
>
> On top of this, you also need to plan your
> engagement time. I set aside half an hour, twice
> a day, every day, where I look at my platforms
> and find opportunities to have conversations
> with people.

Platform Games

One example of how you can use your engagement time is to look on LinkedIn and see who has changed jobs or got a new position. However, rather than sending them the standard 'congratulations', it is better to reach out to them and connect as a human being, which involves some thought. How are you connected to them, what are you congratulating them for, and where are the opportunities? This is for the same reason that I ask people not to send generic messages of congratulations to me.

I have over 8,000 connections on LinkedIn, and so if I have a work anniversary then I will get 5,000 'congratulations'. The problem is that, in amongst those 5,000 responses that are a waste of everyone's time, there will be six people who have actually made the effort to write me a message that has value and is genuinely building a relationship.

This is, after all, the purpose of the platform. Even though I religiously go through all my messages, these personalised messages can sometimes get lost in the avalanche of noise.

The problem is that, if you switch these notifications off so that other people don't see when you have a milestone date, then you limit your visibility – and you want to be seen.

A work anniversary is a really easy way for your profile to get in front of everyone in your network. What they do with the notification is up to them, but maintaining those touch points is really important.

This means that when you are looking at it from the point of view of planning your content strategy, the best thing to do is plan it out platform by platform.

What you need to do on LinkedIn is very different from what you need to do on Twitter or Facebook or

Instagram. You need to be aware of the story you are telling on each platform, who you are talking to, and how you reach them.

Dressing For The Occasion

Using myself as an example, LinkedIn shows a very carefully crafted story of who I am in business. Depending on which industry I am trying to break into, I will tweak my LinkedIn profile by adjusting the type of content that I post.

So if I am sending connection requests to people in the not-for-profit industry, then my profile needs to show that I understand that industry. It needs to give people insight into my experience of working with the industry, and it needs to highlight why we like working for not-for-profit companies.

If my profile is geared towards allied health, for example, then when I send requests to the not-for-profits it may appear as though I don't have a lot of experience working with companies in that area.

By taking a few simple steps, such as reordering your recommendations, you can tailor your profile

to attract the people you are hoping to connect with. It goes back to the idea that LinkedIn is your online dating profile – you always want to dress yourself appropriately to suit the occasion.

Facebook, on the other hand, is very much about customer engagement. You are predominantly talking to your existing customers, and will occasionally have the opportunity to talk to their friends and family.

This makes Facebook a much more relaxed environment. Instagram is different again - it is all about aspirational living, and so you present yet another version of yourself.

Telling The Same Story In Different Ways

Different social media platforms are very much like different social situations offline. The way you behave and the conversations you have when you are at a formal business dinner will almost certainly not be the same as the way you behave and the conversations you have on a night out with your closest friends. It's all still you, but with different aspects brought into play.

So if you asked a stranger who I was and they had only seen my Instagram account, they would say that I travel extensively, enjoy a good single malt whisky, like lifting weights, and read a lot of books. If you asked them the same question based on my LinkedIn profile, you would get a very different summation of my life.

LinkedIn is quite sanitised and very professional. On this platform, you don't want to be the person posting motivational quotes or selfies. LinkedIn is a really powerful tool for building relationships with customers and referral partners, and for having peer-to-peer conversations about trends in your industry.

It is also a great problem-solving tool. Anytime I need a provider or a supplier that I don't have in my network, I'll ask LinkedIn. I will very quickly have a list of thirty recommended people.

I use Instagram to give people some insight into who I am outside of the business. This helps people to feel as though they know me. The advantage of this is that when we sit down and have coffee the speed of trust is brought forward.

It can be time intensive to tailor who you are on all your different social media platforms. However, you can streamline the process by asking what part of the story you are telling, and which version of yourself you are presenting on each platform.

If you are just banging the same thing out across all of your platforms then you are not helping yourself.

People are not on LinkedIn to see the same things they see on Facebook, or on Twitter to see the same things they see on Instagram. In fact, if you look at Australian figures, there are currently 17 million active Facebook users, and only 9 million active users of Instagram.

This means that when you push a post from Instagram through to Facebook with fifteen hashtags and @ symbols, in theory you're creating eight million headaches, because the people who aren't on Instagram don't speak in hashtags and @ symbols. This comes down to lazy use of the platforms.

If you simply want to push your content to all your platforms then you are not having conversations with people - you're shouting at them.

Thumb-Stoppers

When you have someone who manages their social media accounts well, then you tend not to glaze over when their content shows up. Let's say that someone scrolls through 300 feet of Facebook newsfeed every day. The aim is to get them to stop their thumbs. So how do you do that?

One great example of someone managing their LinkedIn account really well is Dr Louise Mahler. She is an international leadership influencer and keynote speaker. She has insightful opinions that she is happy to share, and so when her posts come up on my feed then I tend to stop, because I know she will have something to say that I am likely to find interesting.

Although she does post her own articles, often she will be sharing a piece that someone else wrote. However, she will always say *why* people need to take two minutes out of their life to read what she is sharing.

Social media is one of the places where you can provide insight and value at the start of the purchase process. By doing this, you can circumvent people taking the time to research how they can meet a need.

The aim is to post something that gets my attention. Let's say you're talking about strategic leadership and this is a current challenge that I'm facing in my business. If you post about it then I'm going to come and talk to you. This is because you have given me something which is relevant, and which solves a problem for me.

A good example of this is the people who sign up for multi-level marketing, who are told to get on social media and create content that shows people how to clean make-up brushes or keep food fresh for longer. The people who are successful with this are the ones who teach people new tricks and tips. They provide value, and so people sit up and take notice.

Give A Little, Gain A Lot

Up to a point, providing value is about not being afraid to give stuff away. However, the aim is not to see how many people you can drag into the top of your funnel, throw them through the machine and see who falls out as a bright and shiny new client.

If you place the focus on building relationships with the people you are connected to, so that you are the person they come to when they have a need you can serve, then you place yourself in a very powerful position. To achieve this you can simply provide snippets of advice. You don't need to give away the whole nine yards.

Ultimately what you want to do is to take your online connections and move them offline, so that you are meeting people face-to-face. This is what creates business.

The job of social media is to warm up and nurture the relationship to the point where, when you say, 'Let's catch up for coffee and get to know each other better,' the person you are speaking to says, 'Yes, that would be great.'

So many people get caught up in the idea that they need to be a thought leader. The truth is that thought leaders don't always write everything themselves. Thought leaders are often people who know a lot, and who recognise how a piece of writing connects certain dots.

This means that when they use it as content they can start a conversation. They may achieve this by stating that they agree with the piece, or that they disagree with the piece, but they will always give their reasons, and then ask other people what they think.

How Do You Eat An Elephant?

Knowing what you need to do and how you need to do it is all very well, but it is still very often the case that when you are looking at planning your social media marketing strategy it can be easy to feel overwhelmed.

You need to tailor your content to each platform. You need to plan on a twelve-week *and* a twelve-month cycle. You need to set time aside in your diary on a daily basis for engagement, and a weekly or monthly basis for content planning. Just thinking about it can make your head spin.

In a perfect world, quarterly planning shouldn't be foreign to any business. When you are eating the social media marketing elephant, you can use quarterly planning as your first bite.

Exercise – One Bite At A Time

Keep it simple and go old school. Buy a month-to-a-page wall calendar and write all over it.
As you write you will have ideas. You can then brainstorm and mind-map with post-it notes. You will be amazed at how quickly you can pull together a plan.

Once you have mapped out all of the things that are happening in and around the business over the next twelve-weeks, you can work out which bits will be interesting to your customers. When you have defined this, you can put post-it notes up next to the relevant events.

You can ask which non-competitive connections you have who are aligned with certain events, so that you can engage them in conversations or involve them in promotions. And then you can put post-it notes up next to the relevant events.

You can begin to look at who has the audience that you want to be talking to. What are the big brands and businesses whose posts you can be commenting on. What is your social engagement strategy? And then you can put some more post-it notes up.

You can consider what actions you will take to seek out new potential referral partners and aligned businesses that you're not currently talking to. And then up go some more post-it notes.

Once you have done this you will have your business goals, your content strategy, your social engagement strategy, and your social networking action plan. And suddenly, the elephant has gone.

Example – Planning Ahead

Let's say you are an accountant. You know that financial planners are good for your business. You also know that Google is your friend, so you Google the twenty financial planning offices that are geographically closest to your business.

Once you have your list of twenty businesses, you go into LinkedIn and find out who works in those offices, and then you send a connection request to the most senior person that you can find, using a specific strategy.

The plan is that you are connected to one person in each of those twenty businesses by the end of the quarter. You want to be posting content that is relevant to them, and engaging with the content that they are posting, with the aim that you turn two of those twenty people into a coffee. Your social action plan is actually about social selling.

Once you've got post-it notes outlining your plan, then you just get it all down on paper.

It depends whether you're a list person in a notebook or a task person on the computer, but whatever your mechanism, set up reminders, tasks and to-do lists, and then put all of this into your diary.

Once you've created the plan, execution of the plan is the easy part!

Omnia is a good example of a company who understands how to plan a strategy. The have a whole strategy around 'Feet On The Farm', focusing on which crops are in season.

Through this they guide you towards the products that they create and the issues that they solve for the farmers. The reason this is so clever is that they are wholesalers, so they sell to distributers who then sell to the end user.

However, Omnia understand that they still need to talk to the end user in order to cultivate demand. The important point to understand from this is that your audience isn't always necessarily who you think it is going to be.

So when you are planning you need to think very carefully about who you want to be talking to – with an awareness that this may vary from platform to platform.

In all cases, the key is to remember that you are selling the benefits to the customer. *You are not selling yourself.* Understanding this can help you to be much more comfortable with doing what is required, because it is less about you and more about helping your customer. Most people find it much easier to help others than to talk about how great they are.

Key Takeaways

- If you don't invest in creating a strategy and just 'post stuff', then your content will often be very insipid.

- By incorporating your social media marketing into your overall marketing and communications strategy, and aligning this with your top-line goals, you can create a clearly defined and easily achievable plan that gives you great results with minimal effort.

Chapter Three

Social Media And Face-To-Face Are Not So Different

Although technology has changed rapidly in recent times, the way that we do business hasn't. We still do business with people that we like, know and trust. However, many people create online personas that are very surface-driven, which doesn't help to develop the relationship and build that trust.

Imagine that you're sitting opposite someone having a conversation with them. In this situation, it would not be advisable to talk non-stop about yourself. *The same applies online.*

Once you understand that the way you do business offline is very similar to the way you do business on social media then everything you do online becomes much easier.

Increasing Your Net Worth

For example, suppose that you are a member of a networking organisation, such as Business Network International (BNI). In order to be successful in that networking organisation there are a couple of things you have to do.

Firstly, you need to turn up to all the meetings. Exactly the same principal applies online. **You need to show up on a regular basis.** If you have a heap of social media channels and you never turn up on those channels, then no one is going to see you, and you're not going to be 'front of mind'.

The other thing that you need to do when you are part of a networking organisation is to **be really clear about your referral requests.** You need to know who you want to be introduced to, why you want that introduction, and what it is that you can offer to that person.

Do You Know What You Want?

On social media, people often don't ask for help from their online communities. They're just not very clear with people about what they're trying to achieve. This can be because they don't really know what they are trying to achieve, or it might be because they struggle to ask for help.

Many people go through life not really knowing what they want. They might have an idea that they want more money or more recognition or more success, but because they haven't really defined what that means it is very hard to put it into practice.

Not only this, but from a very young age we are taught not to ask for what we want. In fact, we are often penalised for doing so, by being made to feel weak for needing help, or by being made to feel that we somehow 'owe' the person if they provide us with what we have asked for. All of these things can really get in the way of how we go about doing business.

If you spend time defining exactly what it is you want, and navigate to a point where you make it a habit to ask for those things, then your social media will support this.

Having this clarity gives you the opportunity to be a lot more strategic about how you operate online, because you will know **who you want to connect with, how to go about connecting with them,** and **the types of relationships that you need to cultivate** with those people.

It really is the same as being part of a networking group. You have strategic partnerships with the people who have the same contact spheres as you or who want to engage with the same business types as you. These relationships take greater priority, and you spend more time developing and nurturing them. So why would it be any different online?

Do You Suffer From Premature Solicitation?

Social media is very much about starting the conversation. The mistake that people often make is that they leap straight to premature solicitation, and this doesn't lead to a happy ending for anyone.

You see it on Facebook and LinkedIn in particular. Business people will join groups, and all they ever do is post links to their website or make announcements about the products or services that they're selling.

They're not building relationships with anyone. They

are the person at the party that you're desperately trying to avoid because they've just told you how wonderful they are for the twenty-fifth time. They're not making friends with anyone.

Likewise, on LinkedIn, there are people who send hundreds of connection requests every day. They're playing a numbers game. As soon as someone accepts their connection request, they send through a two-page sales pitch. They copy and paste this pitch and send it through to every single person who accepts their connection request. *That is not how you make friends.*

If I meet you at a networking event, and when I hold out my hand to accept your business card you stuff a two-page proposal into my hand, I'm not going to be signing any cheques made out to your company.

When someone accepts you into their online network, if you take the time to engage with them, comment on their content, and make them feel as though they are your ideal client, referral partner, or prospect, then that's when you can be successful.

Social interaction doesn't come naturally to everyone, and it is fair to say that if you struggle with face-to-face networking then it is likely that you are *really* going to struggle online. *This is because when you take things online mistakes are amplified.*

You can find ways to avoid a lot of the pitfalls, though. The first thing you need to do is understand what they are and why you might fall into them. A great way to do this is to think about things from a DISC profiling perspective.

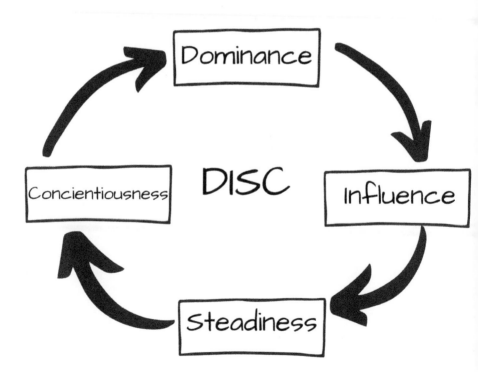

How To Be A Great DISC Jockey

If you meet me face-to-face, it is very clear very quickly that I am predominantly high 'D', high 'I', with very little 'C' or 'S'. So if we meet in person and have a one-to-one conversation you can adapt your communication style to fit this.

You know not to talk to me about the warm and fuzzy things or ask me about my kids, because those are not the conversation I want to have when I'm working.

When you are online, you don't have the advantage of tailoring your communication style to fit one specific person. You're talking to all the different personality types.

You're talking to the detail-oriented 'C' types who read every single word of the Apple user agreement before they click 'yes'. You're talking to the 'S' types who want to know how you go about what it is that you do, what your social impact is, and who you really are. *This means that your content has got to be palatable to everyone.* Very few people consider this when they are putting their content together.

The problem is that **if you try to capture everyone's attention then you will end up talking to nobody.** There are ways you can get around this, though.

By being really clear about the personality types that you work best with, you can tailor your content to connect with those people. For example, in my business, I know that I tend to work best with high 'D' and high 'I' types, as this is how I'm driven. Luckily for me, these people tend to be in decision-making roles, and decision-makers are the people I want to attract.

Tailoring Your Content To Your Audience

The aim is to build a picture of the personality types that are your ideal clients. If you profile your existing 'A' class clients, who are most profitable and take up the least amount of your time, so that you know what their predominant personality type is, then you begin to get an idea of how to package up your content.

So if you want to attract high 'D's, then you need to tell them in the first sentence of your content what it is that you want them to do. Give them the answer straight away. Ensure it is easy for them to make a decision quickly and simply. You don't get many opportunities with the high 'D's.

With the high 'I's, you need to give them a pretty picture or a video, or name-drop someone famous that you've worked with, because the high 'I's are the bright shiny object people who are very easily distracted.

For the 'C' types, you need to include a link to your website, so they can trawl through everything and do their research and due diligence in the way that will help them to feel secure and reassured. And with the 'S' types, you need to talk about how you do what you do.

There is an alternative to profiling your ideal client and aiming the majority of your posts at them. You can ensure that one in every four pieces of content you post is packaged in a way that will appeal to one specific personality type. In this way, you will be giving something to each group. Which gives you a far better chance of getting something in return than not targeting anyone at all.

The various platforms lend themselves to achieving your aims in different ways. For example, with Instagram, the best way of reaching people is to feature a video with a short-form post where people can click the link in the bio to learn more. Knowing this is a great start, but the main point is what you include in the video.

Knowing Where To Focus

I am really big on having a humanist narrative, and being focused on the people in your business. This is because that's what people are actually interested in. When you walk through the door of any business, you want to feel that you know the people you're meeting.

There is room to achieve this in any business, because every business has customer-facing staff. It's not about telling people what each member of your team's favourite colour is or what they like to do at the weekend. *It's about using your people to tell the story of your brand, and to talk about things that your company actually believes in.*

If you are used to being behind the scenes, then

creating videos and posting photos that feature you and your team can feel a bit alien. And if you're not the most socially confident person then it may even feel quite intimidating.

A really good way to overcome these concerns is to ask yourself what you do when you are uncomfortable in face-to-face networking or business situations. Do you talk extensively about all the deals you've closed? Do you name-drop important clients? If you can work out what those hot buttons are, then you can avoid them when you are creating your online content.

The big advantage to creating online content is that you don't ever get put on the spot. You can plan it out and then get someone who is really good with people to give you feedback.

By asking them if the tone you are using is true to who you are and if the content is a good reflection of your organisation, you will get a clearer picture of what you are getting right and where you can make improvements.

Be Unapologetically You

Another point worth understanding is that you don't have to try and emulate the big companies. Running a cheeky Twitter account in the style of Wendy's, for example, may not be the way to go. There are a number of reasons for this.

Firstly, if you are not a naturally funny person then trying to use humour is unlikely to work well for you. However, this leads on to the second point, which is that even if you are amazingly witty but humour is not congruent with your brand then you will either achieve nothing in terms of generating more business or even potentially alienate people.

Having a massive online following might be an ego boost, but if it doesn't do anything to help grow your business, then what's the point?

The other thing to remember is that the big companies have a massive marketing budget and whole teams whose job is to sit on social media and be clever. Small to medium businesses don't have this advantage. *You need to find your own voice.*

When you do you will become the person that people gravitate to, because they will feel the authenticity. So the aim is always to be unapologetically yourself – with the understanding that this should never be at the expense of other people. If you do not engage in a positive and supportive way then it is unlikely you will generate any business from your efforts.

An easy way to achieve this balance is to ensure that when you are on your business channels, you hold in mind the idea that you are having a one-to-one conversation with someone who can change the face of your business. By doing so, you will always be putting your best foot forward.

Dillon's bookshop is a great example of a company striking the right chord. The tone they use is in perfect harmony with their brand, and replicates the feeling you get when you walk into their shop. They post content that not only features books they love and great deals that they are running, but also involves the community.

An example of this is a picture they posted of some chocolate brownies that a customer baked for them.

By including content like this they showcase the positive relationship they have with the people who use their shop.

No matter what you do online, the thought behind it should always be to add value.

Sending out connection requests and then dumping your proposal all over that person as soon as they accept your request is not attractive. Writing insipid comments on people's posts that just say, 'Great article' with a link back to your business page does nothing to build a relationship with that person, and is unlikely to achieve anything for you.

True engagement is key. By giving people insights into who you are, what you believe in, and why, you lay the foundations for a much stronger relationship.

For example, rather than writing 'Great article' you could say 'This is a fantastic article. I really liked the point you made about the impact of sleep on general fitness and recovery.' You could even take it a stage further and ask a question, such as, 'How do you find hydration impacts on recovery times?'

What Are You Building Your House From?

The pace of life in the modern world is hectic. As a result of this, efficiency is given great value. However, the truth is that *faster is not always better*, as we all know from the story of the Three Little Pigs.

This is certainly the case when it comes to social media. Doing something quickly so that you can free up your time for the hundreds of other things that need your attention may seem like a good idea. However, it may not serve you well in the long term.

Going back to the understanding that social media is a tool, there is a difference between *efficient* use of the tool, and *effective* use of the tool. If you spend ten minutes commenting, 'Great article' on ten posts, tick that box and move on with your day then it may be efficient, but is it actually doing anything for you?

If you spend twenty minutes on the same task, taking the time to skim read the articles and extract something that will start a conversation, and *then* comment, you are using the tool effectively.

Social media is not easy to do well, but if you make

an effort with it for a prolonged period of time then you will reap the rewards. In business, you need to be persistent, and social media is no different. You have to be prepared to take the time if you're going to build something solid.

Moving back offline, when you met your best referral partner, the first week after you met them they weren't your best referral partner. It took time to build that relationship.

I have got to the stage with my best referral partner where they can close the deal for me – I don't even need to take the meeting. But it took three years to build to that stage.

Relationship building and earning your credibility is hard work. When you get to the point where people tell you how lucky you are, you know that you've got it right.

I will leave you with this thought. Globally, there are billions of social media users. But no matter how enormous that number is, it will always be made up of individuals.

By remembering that when you go online you are not talking to a faceless machine, you are talking to individual people, you can far more easily become someone that they like, know, and trust.

Key Takeaways

- The way you do business offline is very similar to the way you do business on social media. It's all about developing a healthy relationship based on trust.

- By defining exactly what it is you want, you can be a lot more strategic about how you operate online.

- When you are building relationships, it is far more important to be effective than efficient.

Chapter Four

Your Online Dating Profile For Business – How Do You Scrub Up?

There are a lot of different social networks that you can use, from Facebook to Instagram to Pinterest, but the reality is that these days, LinkedIn is your online dating profile for business. If someone recommends a provider to me, the first place I'll look to find out more about that provider is on LinkedIn.

LinkedIn is really all about **social selling**. It is also the place where people make the greatest number of mistakes. This is because they leap straight to 'buy my stuff'.

The Art Of Social Selling

The understanding of the importance of social selling has been steadily growing for the past couple of years. LinkedIn has a fantastic feature called your **social selling index**, which is a free score that tells you how well you are using the platform.

A really good thing to do before you start editing anything is to check your social selling score, because it gives you a definite point to work from. But before you rush off to look at your score, let's talk about exactly what social selling is.

Social selling is all about taking the pitching component out of the sales process by creating inbound, unsolicited enquiries. This is achieved through the creation of a carefully crafted narrative and content strategy.

Social selling is an art form. The truth is that not everybody is going to like your artwork, but this doesn't mean that you should pack away your paint box.

Your expectation doesn't have to be that everybody will love what you do. It is still worthwhile investing your time in your creations. *But what is it that you are creating?*

With social selling, you are taking the time to create conversations about your products or services that can organically produce sales discussions over time.

To use the real-world analogy, if you are wandering round an art gallery looking at all the exhibits and someone comes up, shoves a painting in your face, and tells you to buy it, it is pretty unlikely they will get a positive response.

Imagine that instead of this they create a space in the gallery to hang their painting. You are able to take the time to sit and admire it. This gives you the opportunity to connect with it and consider what it means to you. As a result, you may well come to the decision that it is something you really want to have in your life.

The Numbers

The reality is that *74% of business-to business buyers conduct more than half of their research online before making a purchase decision or contacting a sales person.* If they are on LinkedIn, then this is one of the places they will naturally turn to.

In Australia there are 4.5 million monthly active LinkedIn users. Since LinkedIn was acquired by Microsoft, more and more Facebook-style functions are being incorporated into the platform.

This means that more and more business conversations are taking place through LinkedIn messaging, rather than more traditional forms of electronic communication, such as email.

Social selling leaders create 45% more opportunities than their peers with lower social selling skills. They are achieving this by using LinkedIn to actively engage with, and expand, their network.

So how do you become one of those leaders? To kick things off, there are some really simple things that you can do to improve your social selling skills.

Exercise - Get Your Profile Looking Hot!

Working from the top of your LinkedIn profile page to the bottom, there are a number of things you can do.

The first thing is to **make sure the banner image that is used by you and all your employees is the same.** And because the whole idea is to create brand congruity, this banner image should be the same as the slider image from your website. In this way, you are instantly recognisable, which gives people the confidence and reassurance that they know who they are talking to.

Another very simple way of improving your social selling is to **make sure that your headline speaks to what people are actually looking for.** If somebody is looking for a social media specialist, they're not going type in 'CEO'. So there is little point in announcing to the world that you are the CEO of your company, if it is not clear what you and your company can do for people.

Contact information is another really simple and straightforward way to increase the likelihood that people will get in touch with you. The number of people on LinkedIn who don't include their contact information is gobsmacking.

If I find you on LinkedIn and you have the capacity to solve a problem for me, then if I can send you an email or call you, I will. At the very least your contact information should include your website and your business landline, but if you are in sales it is a good idea to make your mobile number available too.

Some people don't feel comfortable including their mobile number, but speaking from experience, I have had my mobile number on the platform for eight years and I don't get spammed.

Moving on to **your summary**, I'm a firm believer that this should be structured in a particular way. When we are talking about social selling, **the first two to three sentences should address the pain points that your company solves.** How do you make your clients' lives better, simpler, and easier? You then need to spend a couple of sentences speaking about what you bring to the table that is congruent with that first positioning statement.

Beneath that, **under the guise of 'specialities', you can stuff a whole heap of keywords.** This is very effective, because **your summary is indexable by Google**, as is your headline. This means that if you build your profile properly, it will often outrank your company website.

Once you've tricked out your summary, you can then **add some rich media files.** Uploading pdf files of your products and services, annual reports, images, and whatever else is going to be relevant to your clients, all goes into the 'can't hurt, might help' basket.

If one customer who is going to be worth a great deal of money to your business downloads these files, and this is what gets them over the line, then it will have been worth the five minutes that it took to upload everything.

Remember - the whole purpose of ensuring your profile is as good as it can be is to keep putting drops in the 'yes' bucket.

Once you get down to **your experience,** when you're writing about this from a sales perspective, it is very different from the way you present things when you are job hunting.

Again, the headlines for each of your experience sections are indexable. In fact, *anything you mark to be visible in your public profile will be picked up by Google.* This means that you can begin with another round of keywords before listing your job title. You can then go into more detail about what your current business does.

A good way to break this down is by **size**, **scope**, and **scale**. So you may mention the size of your team, the types of work you like to do, and where you like to do that work. If you hold a lot of board positions, this is the place to include them, and will be particularly attractive to high 'I' and 'S' types.

How much experience is too much?

They say that great art is knowing when to stop, but it can sometimes be difficult to know when you've reached that point. When you are listing your experience on your LinkedIn profile, a good place to stop is with the oldest position you held that still has some relevance to your clients today.

Essentially, you are telling the story of your life in business. You are showing people the skills you have amassed over time and the types of work you have done.

For example, I include in my experience that I was a venue manager for ALH Group. My job was to fix hotels for the company. Although I include this role on LinkedIn, I don't talk about the fact that I can do a stock take.

I talk about the fact that I was a change management specialist, with a successful track record in the areas of business growth, compliance, people development, and culture change. I include these things because they are relevant to my current clients. This means they can look at my LinkedIn profile, see that I've been using those skills for the last twenty years, and subconsciously make a decision that I will have amassed a lot more skills since then.

I don't include that I used to work at McDonald's. However, if I was pitching to McDonald's, then I would absolutely make sure that I included my time there as part of my experience. Because it would have relevance to the company.

Keep in mind that LinkedIn is your business dating profile. If you have something that is going to be attractive to a potential partner which will strengthen the connection, then use it. This includes everything from education to volunteer work.

Once you are confident that you have outlined your experience in a way that highlights everything of relevance that you have to offer, you can move on to your **skills and endorsements.**

Skills and endorsements are like meta tags on a website. If you have ever seen the Encyclopedia Britannica, then your skills and endorsements work in much the same way.

The Encyclopedia Britannica took up an entire shelf, spanning thirty-two volumes, the last two volumes of which were the index. You would go to the index, look up what you wanted to find and the index would tell you which volume you needed. *This is how skills and endorsements work.*

You choose keywords that you use to teach LinkedIn search what you want to be recognised for.

> ## Exercise - Training Montage
>
> You can add up to fifty skills, delete the ones that aren't applicable, and reorder them in a way that makes sense. On LinkedIn, you will often find that you get endorsed by someone you've never met for something that you don't do. *This is because you haven't trained LinkedIn to know what you want to be endorsed for by listing those things in your skills.*

Another way that you can train LinkedIn to recognise where you want to focus people's attention is through the **accomplishments** section. You can list all the different projects that you have worked on, and if those projects have a web presence you can include the links back to the relevant websites.

It's effectively where you can upload all your case studies, with a little blurb about each project. The more projects you list, the more effective they are at guiding people to your profile.

For example, one of the projects I worked on was 'Countering Extremist Violence and Hate Speech

Using Social Media' for the Attorney-General's Department.

The project involved teaching different communities how to create grassroots campaigns to counter the negative narratives they face every day, and helping them to re-engage in a different way.

Including this project in my accomplishments shows that my company is very capable of working on the curlier aspects of things, which is going to be an important piece of information for some of the organisations who are looking for a company to handle their social media.

We All Love The Jam – But Don't Forget The Bread And Butter!

What you are showcasing with your projects is both the biggest, shiniest, brightest jobs that you want to do, *and* your bread and butter jobs. A common mistake that people make on their websites and their LinkedIn profile is to feature only the high-end work.

Although it may look impressive, the result of this can be off-putting to your bread and butter clients, as they are likely to get the idea that you are out of their price range.

You can reorder your projects at any time. If you are trying to break into a particular industry then you can prioritise the work you have done that has relevance to that industry.

This means that when you send a connection request to someone who works in that space and they look at your profile to see who you are and what you do, they will quickly see that you understand how to meet their needs.

Exercise – The Final Bits And Pieces

Once you have uploaded all your projects, the next thing that you want to include are any **certifications** that you or your company holds, along with any **honours or awards**. Anything that you or your company has won or been a finalist in is great to include.

Finally, **Organisations** are memberships that you or your company holds. You should be using them to demonstrate one of three things – experience, success, or relevance.

For example, I am a member of the Australian Marketing Institute. This is the peak body for Australian marketers. This demonstrates my experience, by showing I am a certified practicing marketer, and that I undertake continuous professional development.

Alongside my membership of the AMI, I have shown that my company, Social Media AOK, holds a platinum membership to Brand South Australia. This says that we play at a high level, because there is a certain cost attached to this, and so it shows that the business is established and successful.

The other type of memberships that it is important to showcase are associate memberships of industries that you work with.

I am an associate member of Master Builders Australia -Women In Construction. If I am looking to do more work with people in the building industry, then it reflects positively to be a member of the organisation that they are members of.

When thinking about dressing your profile so that you look your best, this is a little like ensuring your bag and your shoes match the rest of your outfit.

What you really *don't* want to do is have neon green shoes with a bright purple bag. This means it is best to steer clear of organisations with political or religious affiliations.

Not everybody will share your views, and if you limit yourself to creating business opportunities with people who hold all your beliefs, you are quickly going to find yourself staring in the mirror.

So now you've dressed your profile head to toe. You're looking sleek, stylish, warm and approachable. Great! What about the rest of your crew? There's no point making sure you're looking sharp if the rest of your team hasn't made the effort. This is quite an easy problem to solve, though.

It's important that your staff have training on how to use LinkedIn.

It is also important that you have a policy document outlining acceptable use and unacceptable use, and that your sales team has a social networking action plan that builds in KPIs around their activity to make sure they are developing their social selling skills.

Joining The Dots

Having everyone suited and booted is only the beginning, though. The whole point of brushing up your profile is to get a date. This means you need to put yourself out there and build your network.

One of the ways you can go about doing this is to connect with the people you already know. Once you have linked with those people, you can then set yourself some connection targets. After all, nobody starts with thousands of connections!

I have a rule that I will connect with anyone who now, or at some point in the next fifteen years, may need my services or will be able to recommend me to somebody who may need my services. This covers pretty much everyone, because you can't predict where someone will be in fifteen years' time.

Additionally, I will connect with my competitors locally if I've met them and I like them. My view is that there is enough work to go around. I will also connect with my competitors overseas, because companies in the US and the UK are often ahead of the curve.

Working on the principle of six degrees of separation, the more people you are connected to, the closer you are to the people you don't know personally but who you want to have in your network.

Once you begin to grow your network, you can take yourself to the stage where you are only two or three steps away from those people. *This is where the real power is.* It means that you can pretty much type any company name into LinkedIn, see who is working there and what their job titles are, and then begin to form your connection strategy.

How To Make A Connection

When it comes to connecting with people, I am not afraid of hearing the word 'no'. This means that my strategy may make some people uncomfortable, but I find it works well for me.

The first step is to work out who you want to connect to. Let's say that you want to connect to John Smith, who is the CEO of John Smith International. You have a look at his profile, and see that you have eleven mutual connections.

If you look at these eleven connections and work out which person you have the strongest relationship with, you can then pick up the phone and ask them to facilitate an introduction. Remember, social media is a tool. You can't expect it to do all the work for you.

By calling an existing contact you may very well find they are able to make an email introduction so that you can arrange to have a coffee with the person you want to connect with, in order to find out if there is a business opportunity there. This is much more effective than sending your existing contact a message and asking them if they can connect you through LinkedIn.

However, suppose that you don't really know any of your mutual connections well enough to call them and ask for an introduction, or that they don't know the contact well enough to make that introduction. What do you do then?

This is the point at which you can send John Smith a connection request, with a message saying that LinkedIn suggested them as someone you may know.

If you are honest and give them context, by explaining that you haven't actually met, but that you do a lot of work in their industry, then they will be able to begin building trust and see the relevance of connecting with you.

If you let them know that you are always looking to make new contacts in their industry, and that you would be more than happy to connect, if they would like, then you are ensuring they don't feel put on the spot or under any obligation.

Let's suppose that John Smith is a friendly guy and accepts the connection request.

At this point, *you do not hassle him*! This is where so many people go wrong. They make the mistake of thinking that because someone has accepted their connection request they can jump straight to asking for a meeting. You don't want to do this.

What you want to do is have a look at the person's activity feed and begin to comment on the things that they are commenting on, and engaging with the content that they are posting.

People tend not to do this, because they think it seems like a lot of work. My response is to ask the average price tag of an 'A' class client. If a retainer client is worth $50k a year to your business, then why wouldn't you take the time to cultivate the relationship?

One of the things you need to look at is how much of your LinkedIn time you have to convert into clients in order to get a solid return on the investment of that time.

Generally speaking, in the B2B space, the answer will probably be, 'not much'. In the B2C space, if you get one referral partner who ends up sending you four clients a month, then you're home free.

Back to John Smith!

After two to four weeks of engaging with his content, you can then employ a really old-school sales tactic. *You invite him for a coffee.* You do this by sending a LinkedIn message inviting him to meet face-to-face, in four to six weeks time, and saying that you will follow up this invitation with a phone call in a day or two.

The result of this will usually be one of three things. If John Smith is an active LinkedIn user, then you will usually get a response within a couple of hours. There is no guarantee that you will get a positive response, but as a rule active LinkedIn users tend to be happy to meet face-to-face, as they understand this is part of networking.

If the person is not particularly active then you may not get an immediate response. In this instance, you can leave things for a couple of days and then call their office.

If you explain that you are following up on a coffee meeting that you emailed about, then nine times out of ten you will be put through to the person you want to speak to.

You can then suggest a date four to six weeks ahead that you could meet for coffee, and you will usually get a positive response. Few people's diaries are booked out four to six weeks in advance, and so they will almost certainly have availability. This timeframe may seem excessive, but when getting your LinkedIn business date, you're playing the long game.

Once you have secured your coffee meeting, you come to the all-important part! You've actually made it to your business date! This is exciting! However, this is where people tend to trip over themselves, because they spend the entire meeting talking about themselves.

This first coffee together is not the meeting where you want to turn up with a proposal document or a ton of manila folders full of bright glossy brochures.

The smart thing to do at this point is to make friends. Spend the first thirty minutes asking about the other person. Ask them questions that people don't normally ask. Take the time to find out what their challenges are and what they enjoy about their role.

To give you an example of how this can work, I met a guy who was an ISO certified quality manager. I asked him what the most bizarre job was that he'd had to do accreditation for. Nobody had ever asked him that before, and his eyes lit up as he began telling me about the time he'd had to go to a snake venom factory. Instantly, we had a rapport.

If you ask your business date about themselves diligently for thirty minutes, then there will come a point where they then ask about what you do. *This is not when you launch into what you can do for them!*

By simply talking about what you love, the challenges within your organisation, and by giving them a couple of tips and tricks that will be helpful to them, you build the foundations of a solid relationship.

If the person has an immediate need, they will probably let you know. If this is the case, ask to make a separate sales meeting in order to have those discussions.

By not selling to the person in this initial meeting, they are much more likely to trust you, and also much more likely to recommend you to others.

Once you have had this meeting, follow up. Send them a note thanking them for taking the time to meet. If possible, see if you can find another way to connect. Invite them to an event or a business lunch that has relevance to what they do.

Continue to develop the relationship and strengthen the connection. After all, **the whole point of having a great business dating profile is to create great business relationships.**

Key Takeaways

- By taking the time to create conversations about your products or services, you can organically produce sales discussions over time.

- When you take the time to get your LinkedIn profile looking hot, you give out clear signals about who you are and what you do.

- Don't leap straight to premature solicitation! Taking things slowly with new connections will build trust and create a solid foundation to your relationship.

Chapter Five

You Look Hot So Now What? – Connection Strategies

There is absolutely no point in having a magnificent LinkedIn profile and being really engaged on your Facebook business page if you don't have a clear understanding of what it is you're trying to achieve.

When it comes to social media, the biggest mistake that businesses make is not developing a clear understanding of who their ideal clients and referral partners are. Because they don't know who they want to focus on, they take a machine gun approach in the hope that a bullet will land somewhere. That's never going to end well.

Creating Client Connections

To resolve this problem, the first thing you need to do is take a close look at your business, so you can work out who your 'A' class clients are.

These are the ones who take up the least amount of your time, make you the most money, and who are stickier - so that they stay with you for a long time. Once you have defined who these clients are, consider what it is that you know about them.

Example – Building Healthy Relationships

Suppose you are an accountant, and that you specialise in working with doctors. You know that specialists, surgeons, GPs and consultants are your ideal clients. You value them because they are busy professionals, and so they just let you get on with your job.

If you know that these people are your ideal clients, you can develop a strategy to connect with more of them. You might start by going onto LinkedIn and searching for a big private hospital close to your business. By looking on the hospital's company page you can see exactly who works there.

At this point you don't want to leap to premature solicitation. It is far better to begin by grooming your profile a little bit. So you might want to make sure that one in three articles you post on LinkedIn are about accounting challenges for healthcare professionals.

These could be things such as 'Five Mistakes Doctors Make When They Hire An Accountant'. It would also be a good idea to make sure that you have recommendations from some of your existing clients in healthcare. At this stage, you're making sure you look the part.

Once you have groomed your profile, you can formulate a prospect list. This would include the name of the person, where they work, what mutual connections you have, what they are interested in, what they are commenting on, and what seems to get their attention.

> If they are in any of the same groups as you then you can begin commenting in those groups, and from there you can get to a point where you send them a connection request. *You need to understand who you are talking to before you make direct contact with them.*

With A Little Help From Your Friends

As we have seen in the previous chapter, you can circumvent a lot of pain if you've got a mutual connection that you know really well. Something that is often overlooked when we are using social media is that you can step out of the online world and pick up a telephone to call someone.

If you call your friend and ask them how well they know Dr Green, then you might discover that they went to school together and their families take annual skiing holidays with each other. If this is the case there is a strong chance they will be able to facilitate an introduction.

Alternatively, your friend might confess that they have never actually met Dr Green, and that they are just connected on LinkedIn. This means they won't be able to help you, but you will have ticked off the box of taking the most direct route.

It is worth noting that if you are looking for an introduction from a mutual connection it is far better not to send an email, but to actually pick up the phone and speak to your friend.

It can be perceived as rude to send an email asking for a favour. *The relationship is always more important than the sale.* The minute you put a potential sale ahead of an existing relationship, everything begins to fall down.

Direct Contact

Let's say you have been unsuccessful in finding a mutual connection who can make the introduction. At this point you can send the person a message with a note saying that LinkedIn suggested them as someone that you might know. It is important to be honest and acknowledge that you haven't met, but if you have mutual connections it is absolutely fine to point this out.

Let them know that you are always looking to expand your network and that you would be more than happy to connect with them. Ensure you make it clear that this is only if they would like to, so that they can make a decision without feeling pressured. Eight times out of ten they will accept your request. After all, everyone is on LinkedIn to do business.

Being really clear about who you want in your network and then connecting to those people is your primary consideration. Alongside this, making a habit of connecting on LinkedIn with everybody that you physically meet is also important.

If your profile is optimised for your ideal client and tells them how you solve their problems, then that profile is going to pre-qualify your customers.

This means that if you go and have a coffee with someone, and then subsequently send them a LinkedIn request, it is only natural for them to have a look at your profile. If your profile is red hot, then you might get a second date – and it certainly can't hurt.

Thinking Ahead

If your connection strategy is sales driven, so that you connect with anybody who either now or at some point in the future may need to use your services, or who can refer you to people who might need your services, then you greatly increase your chances of finding the people who you can do business with.

This may sound as though you're looking to connect with anyone and everyone, but you can still be selective within these broad parameters. It's just good to bear in mind that people change jobs and even industries much more frequently these days.

The other advantage to thinking ahead is that you can also ensure you connect with people at a junior level. This means that by the time they begin to climb the corporate ladder and move into decision-making positions, you have already established a relationship with them.

It's all about anticipating possibility. Just because someone is working in a bar today, it doesn't mean that they aren't going to be the CEO of a major corporation in ten years' time. If you've been connected for ten years and they have been seeing your content throughout that time, then you are absolutely going to be their first port of call.

My experience is that some of my best clients have come from this process. I connected to a gentleman who, at that time, taught Occupational Health and Safety at TAFE in Melbourne. This was six or seven years ago, when I was in registered training.

I went off and started my company, and he continued to pursue a career in health and safety. He ended up as the CEO of a global safety company, delivering training all around the world.

Out of the blue, I got a message from him saying 'Hey Simone, when are you next in Melbourne? We need to talk.' *Because I had been consistently front-of-mind for what I do, with no white noise, he knew exactly where to turn when he needed the services my company offers.*

Balancing Act

In terms of what you post, **your content plan should be geared towards the verticals that you are going**

after at any specific time. When you are actively looking to break into a particular industry your content will lean towards attracting those people, but you should still be posting about other things too.

By ensuring your content achieves multiple aims – reaching specific audiences and providing value for a wider range of demographics – you can ensure you retain everyone's interest even during the times when your focus is in one particular direction.

There are always opportunities to write general articles that are designed to educate clients. *And because the articles stay on your profile, it is effectively an embedded blog.*

If you don't have access to a website it is a really great place to position yourself as someone who has useful things to contribute. Additionally, your LinkedIn content is shareable across all your other platforms, so you can reach wider audiences, and also attract people to your LinkedIn profile from other platforms.

So this is the process when looking to attract direct clients. **The most important point to remember**

is that you are very careful not to try and sell to them. However, the more of them you can accumulate as connections, the better. This is because they will consistently see your content, and so when they have an explicit need, they are more likely to reach out to you.

Referral Partners

When it comes to referral partners, it is a completely different ballgame. **With your referral partners, the focus needs to be on staying front-of-mind** *for the right reasons.* This is where social proofing comes in.

Social proofing works on the principal that when somebody is unsure about something, they will look to others for guidance about what they should do.

When you are trying to attract referral partners, and they have little or no knowledge about who you are or what you do, they are likely to look for confirmation of your abilities from other people who they deem to have more knowledge and information.

So where do they get this knowledge and information? *They get it from your existing referral partners* - through recommendations those existing partners have left on your LinkedIn profile.

Example – The Proof Of The Pudding

A mortgage broker is a fantastic referral partner for an accountant. Let's say the accountant has three to six mortgage brokers currently referring them work. Imagine that all of those mortgage brokers have left recommendations on the accountant's profile talking about how amazing and brilliant they are.

The accountant then sends requests to other mortgage brokers. They can see that this person is already endorsed by a number of mortgage brokers. This means they are far more likely to be interested in connecting. *This is social proofing.* It is very simple, and it is very powerful.

Making The Time To Grow Your Network

Understanding how to achieve your aims is the first step. The next step is to diarise time so that you can execute your strategy. *Connections require attention and nurturing.*

For instance, you need to check every day to see who has looked at your profile. And then you need to make sure you have sent them a connection request. Once again, this requires putting some thought into how you go about making friends and winning people over, which will vary from person to person.

Let's say that one of the people who looked at your profile is someone who has a quote from you sitting on their desk. The first thing you need to do is pick up the phone and call them.

If they've already got a quote and they're looking at your profile, then they are making up their minds. If they are making up their minds and they've got three quotes on their desk, then by ringing and asking if they've got any questions, you automatically put yourself in front of everybody else.

Another person who looked at your profile might be someone who you know really well but haven't seen for ages. Again, this is a great opportunity to pick up the phone or send them an email letting them know that you'd love to catch up with them.

Sometimes their response will be that they have been meaning to get in touch with you because they need your services. This is why they were looking at your profile in the first place.

You will also have people looking at your profile because you have come up in LinkedIn search. You have no connection to them, but they look like they would be a good person to have in your network.

This is when you can employ the tactic of sending them a connection request and a personalised message to say LinkedIn put them forward as someone you might know and you'd be happy to connect with them. This is likely to get a more positive response than letting them know that you saw they'd been looking at your profile.

Everything you do needs a slightly different approach, just as it does in the real world. This is for the same reason that, in spite of the fact you have a faceless screen in front of you, *every single connection you make is to an individual*, and the relationships we have with each and every person in our lives is unique.

Supersize Me?

The connection strategy that you use needs to be consonant with who you are and what you do. However, it is worth considering a couple of points. There are two schools of thought when it comes to how you make connections on LinkedIn.

The first is based around the original LinkedIn model, which is to only connect with people that you have actually done business with. This creates a small, tight, closed network.

LinkedIn's rules around sending connection requests have relaxed a little over the years. Although you are still not encouraged to send requests to people you don't know, and will in fact be blocked from inviting people to connect if you send too many of these requests, the policy is not as stringent as when the platform was first created.

There may be advantages to keeping your network very exclusive, but it is not necessarily going to help you maximise your opportunities. One example that comes to mind is a lawyer who worked for a very large law firm.

Example - Closed For Business

LinkedIn had rules in place about only connecting with people you knew. In spite of this, the lawyer had included in his profile that he would only connect with people that he had met, and that if you wanted to send him a connection request you would need to state where you had met him.

At the time, because he was working for such a large company, he didn't really need to look for new clients or think about business development. This meant it didn't matter if he seemed a little self-important and kept his network very tight.

Fast-forward a couple of years, and this lawyer had gone out on his own. Suddenly

> business development became far more important, and he needed to reframe and reassess his connection strategy.

There is nothing wrong with having closed networks if that is what works for you. Some people are never going to be comfortable having big networks. However, when it comes to social selling, if you want to be successful you need to give yourself the best chance.

There are a few things that will really help. **You need a really broad network. You need a strategy for tapping that network on the shoulder on a regular basis. And you need a strategy for creating opportunities for people from that network to meet you face-to-face.**

This means reaching out and inviting people to do things with you. It doesn't only have to be coffee. If you see a good networking event with a keynote speaker that you think would be of interest to one of your referral partners, call them and ask them along.

To a great extent, we've forgotten how to be

social. Things that happened quite naturally before the internet and social media existed now require thought and planning.

It is for this reason that having connection strategies is crucial if you want to break down those barriers, attract new clients and referral partners, and move your business forward. It is all about giving people value.

Keep Your Eyes On The Prize

When you sit down and you work on your connection strategy, you need to consider what your KPIs are. You should have a social networking action plan, with KPIs attached to it. You should know how many ideal clients you need to connect to on LinkedIn.

Let's say you need to connect with twenty doctors this month in order to secure two coffee meetings. If you have two coffee meetings every month, then you can reasonably expect one of those two people to turn into a client. Therefore, within a year, you will have developed a strategy that gives you twelve new clients.

The other really important point here is to understand what can go wrong when building your connection strategy and reaching out to new connections.

The first question you can ask yourself is whether you are actually interested in the person you are reaching out to. If you're not, that is a good indication that you've leapt to the end of the whole process, rather than starting at the beginning.

You can easily overcome this problem by asking yourself what you know about that person. Do you know what they are interested in, passionate about, what they're engaging with?

Example - What's Hot And What's Not

I recently received a connection request from a culinary coach hospitality strategist. I accepted the request. The following morning I received a message thanking me for connecting.

He then went on to ask me if there was anything I needed to know or any more information I needed about his business and services. He said that, even though he wasn't sure how he could help me, if there was anything he could do for me that he would be more than happy for me to contact him.

He sent me a connection request, and then asked what he could do to help me. To use a Tinder analogy, he swiped right on my profile. I had a look, and swiped right on his profile too, so that we were a match.

However, because he hadn't spent any time looking at my profile, he then sent me a message asking if I like long walks on the beach or dancing at nightclubs. *He had no idea what he could offer me, because he had no idea who I was and what I was looking for.* The answers to all the questions he was asking me were in my profile.

There are people who do it really well, though. A woman recently sent me a connection request, which I accepted. She then followed this up with a short message, thanking me for the presentation that I had given the day before, saying that she had felt inspired and invigorated, and had really enjoyed both the content and the delivery of the presentation.

She didn't ask me for anything. She recognised that it was more important to begin building the relationship, and that we weren't going to get into business bed together straight away.

It is often men who leap straight to trying to close the deal. There are many books out there talking about how men are better at closing the deal. This may well be a gross generalisation, but it does come up time and again as a theme in a wide number of business books.

The reason for this seems to be that men are more comfortable hearing the word 'no'. This means that they will ask for the sale, hear the word 'no', and then move on and ask for the sale from someone else.

Some women, on the other hand, tend to analyse the situation. They try to work out what they did wrong, and end up overthinking it. Somewhere in the middle is the best of both worlds.

What You Give Is What You Get

To occupy the middle ground when you are creating your connection strategy, you need to ensure you are constantly doing two things. **Always looking to connect, and always looking to offer value.**

Consistently offering value in the content that you share and the articles that you write will, over time, generate the inbound sales enquiries you are looking for.

On top of this, having a wide network that you don't spam is a very powerful tool. *As you develop that network and deepen their trust, they begin to solve your problems for you, as well as generating sales.*

How your network solves your problems can be just as important for your business as the work they generate. For example, I used to chair the State Advisory Committee for the Australian Marketing Institute in South Australia. We were having 'The Great Marketing Debate', and four weeks before the event was due to take place, an entire team dropped out.

I posted on LinkedIn, asking for people who were at the top of their game in marketing who would be interested in taking part in the debate. Within two hours, I had eighty six comments, and within three hours I had a brand new debating team, and my problem was solved. If I had tried to achieve the same results by phone, it would have taken days.

When you position yourself in such a way that you're creating space to make connections, and then navigate to a point of trust, you can benefit in so many ways.

Alongside generating sales and solving your problems, having a broad network can be a fantastic way to carry out market research, and help you to find out what the pain points of your clients and potential clients are, because you have a window into their worlds.

A great connection strategy opens up so many doors, and the rewards that lie behind these doors make it well worth the time and effort it takes to unlock them.

Key Takeaways

- When you take the time to develop a clear understanding of who your ideal clients and referral partners are, you are able to focus your energy in the right direction

- When you work on your connection strategy, consider what your KPIs are. You need to know what you are aiming for.

- Your network can do so much more than generate sales. They can solve your problems and give you insight into what your clients need.

Chapter Six

Personal Brand Versus Company Brand - How To Harness Both

When it comes to social media, a company brand is exactly what you imagine it to be. There will be a company Facebook page, company LinkedIn page, company Twitter account and so on.

This is all very straightforward. In an ideal world, alongside your brand, your company has its own humanistic narrative, telling the story of your company's vision, values and ethics.

But what about your personal brand?

Throughout my twenties I worked for a very large company, Australian Leisure and Hospitality Group. I worked for them while Foster's owned them. I worked for them through a takeover. I worked for them when they became independent, and I worked for them when Woolworth's took them over.

During this entire period of time, I thought that I had a personal brand. I had been working for the company for nine years, and I knew heaps of people. *What I didn't realise was that when you leave a big company, pretty much all of those connections fall away.* This is where things like LinkedIn and Facebook come in handy.

Do You Know What Your Personal Brand Is?

Your personal brand is very much about who you are within the company, and how you choose to share the content from the company – how you choose to appear as a brand ambassador for your company.

When you are a business leader you're leading by example. *CEOs often make the mistake of thinking that, because they are the chief executive officer, they don't need to be on social media.*

The head of one of the biggest companies in Australia recently told me that he didn't need to be on LinkedIn, because if someone didn't have his contact details then it meant they weren't meant to have them.

From a personal perspective, this may be a fair point. *But how does it help the company?* How does it help all your staff who are out there trying to sell? The truth is that **the more you cultivate your relationships and support your staff to achieve the goals they are trying to achieve, the better it is for your business.**

Richard Branson is a great example of a leader who ensures he stays very connected with his audiences, even if all he really wants to do is stay on his private island. Many of us can relate to this desire.

I am an adaptive introvert. I can 'people' at a large scale for a very short time, and do it very well, and then I need to build a blanket fort. So even the most reluctant social butterflies can cultivate the skills that allow them to be social. By doing this, you can then take those skills and apply them online.

How Do You Uncover What Your Personal Brand Is?

In addition to these social skills, when it comes to creating your own personal brand, there are a couple of things that you need to understand. Firstly, **you need to ensure that the story you are telling aligns with the story the company is telling.** Part of ensuring this happens is understanding that we all make a choice in life.

When I used to fix broken hotels I would always ask the staff to write me a letter, outlining three things. Firstly, why they chose to work at the venue, when they could work in any number of other places. Secondly, what they loved about the venue that they didn't want to see changed, and why. And finally, what they couldn't stand about the venue and how they would fix it.

After completing this task something really interesting would happen. Within two weeks, anyone that needed to leave resigned - all by themselves.

This was because I had pointed out to them that they were making a choice to work at that venue.

Once they thought about that choice, they could quickly see if it was really what they wanted to be doing.

The other thing that would happen which was really interesting was that that I would get amazing feedback about the culture of the venue. This gave me a clear idea about what I needed to look after, in order to hold onto the staff that needed to stay. I also got some great insights into how to fix the underlying problems in the organisation.

This exercise is really powerful, and applies equally when you are thinking about the choices that you make when being a brand ambassador for your company.

Why do you have the business that you have? Why do you work where you work? What is important to you about working there, and what is the story you need to tell about it?

What Is The Story I Should Be Telling?

Even though you are creating your own personal brand, the story you tell is not how amazing and fantastic you are. Because no one cares. Really. And nor should they! **When it comes to your company narrative you are not the hero of your story.** *Your customer is.*

It is all about what the customer wants, what the customer needs, and how you can make it straightforward for the customer to give you money. That's the journey you want to take people on.

In order to harness your personal brand you need to be really clear about what you bring to the table. What is your role within the organisation, what do you contribute to the organisation, and what are you supporting the organisation to achieve?

Once you have worked this out, you can make some really clear choices about the types of content that you share from the organisation - and the way that you share it.

All of a sudden, your content becomes much more purposeful, and once this happens you connect on a human-to-human level, *because you are explaining to your audience what it is that you do for them, and why.*

Example – ANZAC Day

The Duke of Brunswick rarely opens on public holidays, but we do open on ANZAC day. When I talk about the fact that we are open on ANZAC day, I explain it in a way that connects me to my customers.

I let them know that my grandfather was one of the Rats of Tobruk and was in the 2/10th battalion. I tell them that my grandmother served in the army, and my mother served in the navy. And whilst I chose not to serve, I make it clear that I appreciate the sacrifice of those who have given so much, so that we, as a nation, don't have to sacrifice very much at all.

The point of this is that **there is a transparency and a narrative that sits behind this that has nothing to do with marketing.** *It is about who I am and who the organisation is.*

Working Out Your Narrative

This is what you have to get clear. What is your narrative? When you make a business decision there is always a narrative that sits behind it, but as a rule we don't spend very much time interrogating it.

This is where making sure your personal values are aligned with your company values comes into play. There's no point in heading up a vegan food chain and then posting a picture of a big, juicy steak.

Of course, it is much easier as the business owner to ensure your personal values and your business values occupy the same space, because the business is driven that way.

Having said this, some business owners create their business values based on what they think is going to be well received by their audience, even though it is not really in line with their personal values. When this happens, they often create a bit of a psychological bump for the people around them, including on social media.

So if your posts position you in one space, and

then when people meet you there is a gap between those posts and who you are in the real world, then things won't feel right. **When it comes to representing your values and your company's values, you can't pay lip service.**

The digital world is absolutely an extension of who you are - *when you do it well!* However, when you do it badly it is nothing more than a representation of who you think other people want you to be, and they will quickly figure that out.

Getting Comfortable In Your Niche

When you're not concerned about external validation then you are much more comfortable being honest about who you are, and the right people will gravitate to you. To a great extent, this comes back to understanding your niche. Many business owners are terrified to niche.

The thinking is that, if someone falls broadly into the spectrum of needing your services, you should be attracting them to your company. Social Media AOK is a great example of why you don't need to do this and how niching can work.

Example - AOK With Who We Are

At Social Media AOK we don't try to attract every single person who wants an online presence. From the very beginning, all we have done is social media marketing.

We don't do web design. We don't do branding. We don't do web hosting. Our point of difference is that we focus very specifically on sales and top-line business goals – so all our energy goes into getting you to where you want to be.

There is value in working with people who are happy to say that they specialise. *If you're really clear on what it is that you do for your clients and how you help them, then you're going to be very comfortable having an opinion on things.*

People want to benefit from your expertise, and so being able to confidently voice your opinion on what is and isn't going to work for your clients will always be extremely valuable to them. My caveat to that is that you deliver your opinion in a way that is kind.

I have a really simple health check for this. At Social Media AOK our mantra is that we're seriously social, and that business always starts with coffee.

We never send out quotes to clients without having a coffee with them first. This means that I get a lot of people messaging me on LinkedIn and Facebook asking if we can have a coffee. This is where the health check comes into play.

As your business grows, your time becomes very valuable. It can become hard to make time for all those cups of coffee! However, I don't know anything about the people requesting coffees! I don't know who they are, who they know, what they can teach me, where their life has been, or where they're going.

As a result of this, I have told my team that if the day comes when I say I'm too busy to go for a coffee with someone, they have permission to slap me. *This is because in order to stay aligned with my personal values and my company values I always need to make time for everyone who expresses an interest in my business.* The same applies to all businesses.

Are Your Feet Too Big?

With this in mind, when you are massaging your personal brand, if someone takes the time to comment on an article that you posted or a piece of content that you shared, it is important to take the time to engage them in conversation and to value their opinion. *No matter how big your feet are, make sure they are never too big for your boots.*

You really do need to put thought into how you represent yourself and your brand in everything that you do.

Example – Taken Out Of Context

One of my referral partners recently liked a photo on LinkedIn that didn't strike me as being appropriate. I'm not even sure what it was doing on LinkedIn. It was a very provocative picture of a woman in a nightclub wearing a very low-cut dress. Because he liked it and we are connected, it came up in my feed.

Because kindness is key, I didn't cause him embarrassment by publicly distancing myself from him. I didn't comment on the image to say I thought it was inappropriate. Instead, I sent him a private message asking why he had liked the photo, as it didn't seem to be aligned with my understanding of who he was or what his personal values were.

He explained that the photographer was a friend of his, and that was the reason he had liked the picture. I asked if he would like some feedback that would potentially make him more money. He said yes, absolutely.

I explained that when the photo came through my feed I could have made the judgement that he had liked the photo of the young girl in a skimpy dress because he was a lecherous man. If I hadn't known him better that would have been the judgement I made. And it would have impacted on whether or not I chose to refer to him.

I explained that because I knew him I had

messaged him to get context, and that I now understood that he was supporting his friend, but most of his connections wouldn't have any context, and the flow-on effect was likely to be that they would make a negative judgement about him.

He was very appreciative of the feedback. **When you are thinking about your personal brand, context is always going to be of paramount importance.**

Shout Out To Your People

Building up a really solid personal brand presence allows you to amplify the company's brand. Employee advocacy is one of the big ticket items of the year, and it is a great way to increase that amplification.

The reason for this is that your team are much more likely to engage with *their* personal brand when you lead from the front. This is where things like giving LinkedIn 'kudos' come in. If it is done with meaning, giving kudos can be a really useful tool.

I recently had a notification from LinkedIn suggesting that I give one of my staff kudos, because she had been with the company for a certain amount of time. I was happy to do this, but I couldn't give it the attention that I needed to at that moment, so I waited until I was on my lunch break and I could write a message that had meaning.

Rather than just saying, 'Kudos to Payam for being with Social Media AOK for two years', I let her know that she was an invaluable member of the team and that I really appreciated her diligent attention to detail when it came to creating our clients' content.

It's very similar to the automatic 'congratulations' that get sent out when people have work anniversaries or new positions. **By being the person who takes the time to connect, rather than just giving the standard response, you will be the one who stands out from the faceless crowd.**

Are You On The Right Track?

Your personal brand takes time to build. It's really just another word for credibility. You don't just snap your fingers and suddenly you have a great personal brand.

It's just not how personal branding works. *You need to consistently apply a strategy using the tools available.*

At first, it may seem as though you're not getting any traction. It's important not to feel disappointed if this is the case. Instead, ask yourself a couple of questions. If it's an article that you've written, then ask yourself if you're providing value or if you're selling.

If you're selling and no one is engaging, then that's not surprising. If you are providing value and no one is engaging, then you can consider whether or not you got your headline right. **You always need to be looking at yourself rather than the rest of the world, to see what you can change for the better.**

Tag Team

Another point to consider is in relation to the recent trend of tagging multiple contacts if you want your post to reach further in a shorter timeframe. The problem is that it has no context.

I will often get tagged in something and then when I look at it, there is no relevance to who I am or what I do. And then, because twenty other people are tagged in the post, I get endless notifications about the comments they are posting.

It's ok to tag people in your posts, but **tag selectively**! If you have found something that you really believe will be of interest to someone, then an even more effective strategy than tagging is to *send that person a private message with a link.*

Let them know that you found the article interesting and ask them what they think. This is so much better than just shoving your brand into their connections' news feeds.

If you send a private message, good manners will dictate that the person will at least respond, even if they didn't find the article interesting. If nothing else, you have opened a dialogue with that person.

It's all about behaving in the way that you behave in the real world. For the simple reason that it's the same. You're still dealing with a person - it's just through a keyboard rather than face-to-face.

We forget this, because we get so caught up with

trying to meet our own needs and wants. As a result we just tick all the boxes as quickly as possible, which goes back to efficient versus effective.

If you tag twenty people in your post, and this gives you a reach of 20,000 people but no one engages with it, and you've irritated twenty key people in your network in the process, then you haven't done yourself any favours – even if it did seem really efficient.

It always comes back to a few very simple points. By considering who you are, what you stand for, how you can provide value to your network, and how can you personalise that process, you will build a personal brand that truly resonates with your audience.

Key Takeaways

- The more you cultivate your online relationships and support your staff to achieve their goals, the better it is for your business.

- The digital world is an extension of who you are. By being honest about who you are, the right people will gravitate to you.

- It takes time to build your personal brand. By consistently applying a strategy using the tools available, you will develop a narrative that truly represents who you are, and perfectly aligns with your company's aims.

Chapter Seven

Playing The Long Game In An Instant Gratification Society

When people start using social media for business there is often a gaping chasm between expectation and reality. The expectation is that the moment they start posting content everyone will share and like and comment, so that all their brilliant insights and witty memes go viral.

After this happens, the money fairy will bring them all the dollars and the world will rejoice. When they find out that the reality doesn't match up, it often leads to a level of disinterest and disharmony within the business.

Getting Comfortable In Your Surroundings

Using social media for business is about cultivating long-term relationships. Once you understand this it becomes much easier to feel comfortable with the fact that you probably won't know how those relationships are going to benefit your business for some time. This is true whether you are using Facebook, Instagram, LinkedIn or Twitter.

On all of these platforms your followers are your advocates. However, *they are only able to step into this role when there is an opportunity for them to do so.* Just asking them to comment, share and tag does not make them brand advocates.

Being really clear about the value you are offering to your audiences is key. When you're playing a long game then you are consistently looking at how you have achieved this.

You are thinking about what you have done each week to demonstrate size, scope and scale. You are considering the ways in which you have reminded your wider network what it is that you do, without selling to them.

This is the definitive point. **You're not selling to the people directly in front of you. You're selling to the 150 people in the networks that sit behind each of those people.**

Constructing Meaningful Relationships

Dunbar's Theory says that we can comfortably maintain 150 stable relationships where we know who each person is and how all of those individuals relate to one another. In essence, those 150 people are your network.

However, the truth about social media is that we have many more contacts than these 150 meaningful relationships. I have over 8,500 connections on LinkedIn. I have over 2,000 'friends' on Facebook, over 1,000 followers on Twitter, and a similar number on Instagram. Those are my personal accounts.

For the most part, these people are not my friends in the traditional sense of the word. I can count the number of people I consider to be real friends of the fingers of one hand, or two at a stretch. It's fair to say that this is true for most people.

What this means is that we have a high number of surface relationships, because social media has blurred the boundaries between all the different areas of our lives.

Education, Education, Education

As a result, it is important to understand you are educating the people you have these surface relationships with *all the time*. Everything you do online builds a picture of the type of person you are, who you are in business, what you do and the problems that you solve.

The way you achieve this is through storytelling. Putting up links to your website every week is not going to get you the results you are looking for.

The Lost Art Of Storytelling

One of the roadblocks that people run into when they are using social media is that not everybody is good at telling stories. Most people know someone who is a magnificent storyteller, who has you hanging on every word.

Sadly, this is not a skill that we teach people any more. Not only this, but the way we digest information has changed, and no longer lends itself to storytelling.

This is because mobile phones dictate that information is now packaged in sentences rather than paragraphs. As a result, our brains now process information in much smaller, bite-sized pieces.

In spite of the difficulties surrounding storytelling, it is the most effective way of reaching people. Which means there is one fundamental question you need to ask yourself in order to be successful at social media. **What is the story that you are telling about your company?**

In order to answer this question, you need to be clear about a few things. *You need to understand your company values, what you do, how you do it, and the part each of the people within your business play.* Once you have clarified these points, you can then think about how you tell your story to the world.

Can They See The Real You?

People are demanding more and more transparency and accountability from businesses. This means that the things they are really interested in are what you care about, other than making money. *The people who are most successful are the ones who have a really clear narrative about what they stand for and what's important to them.*

This is a foreign concept for a lot of businesses. Pretty much every single business was founded because somebody was good at something, and didn't want to work for someone else. For the majority of these business owners, the thing that they are really good at is not marketing or storytelling. It is electrical work or carpentry or massage or medicine.

Even so, there are many examples that demonstrate you don't need a background in marketing to be great at social media.

Example – A Bright Spark

There is an electrician in Adelaide, Matt Downie from iElectrical and Communications, who does a fabulous job. Social media marketing is the only marketing he does. In the space of two years he has gone from being a sole trader to having a team of four other electricians working for him.

The reason why he does social media so well is that he tells the story of the way iElectrical go about doing things, not what it is that they do. And people are far more interested in finding out about the team than about the wiring. After all, if you get an electrician, you expect them to do the electrical stuff.

This means that when he posts pictures of sites they are working on, and everything is neat and clean, his audience get an insight into how tidy his team are when they are working.

And when he runs a competition for his customers to send in pictures of their weirdest light fittings, he gives his audience a chance to connect with one another, and also offers a humorous glimpse into the kinds of things he and his team encounter when they are on the job.

This means that people who see his posts are more likely to choose him over any other electrician. It is clear to see that he cares about his customers, his team, his young family, and his reputation in the marketplace. Through great storytelling he transforms a dry topic into engaging content.

Being seen is something that many people are not comfortable with. However, when you are using social media it is crucial that you are seen as a human being. This comes back to the simple truth that people do business with people.

Example - Let The Sun Shine In

A great example of how this works in the real world is the advertising boards that Australian estate agents put up when they are selling houses. In many countries, these boards only feature the name and contact details of the agency selling the property. In Australia, the boards also feature a larger than life interior shot of one of the most attractive parts of the house, and a photo of the agent handling the sale.

By letting people see into the home, they are immediately able to understand the ways in which they will benefit from that purchase. By including an image of the agent, potential buyers know who will guide them through the purchase process.

Rather than a plain board stating that the house is for sale, there is **insight, context, relevance,** and **the foundation of a relationship.** The agency has told a story. *Social media works in exactly the same way.*

Keep It On The Level

One point that should be very clear is that **the story you are telling needs to be true.** It's all very well saying your values are that you're friendly and ethical. However, this becomes meaningless if your staff are rude to your customers, or your product is known to damage the environment.

It's great to want to tell a good story. *The problem is that if the story does not accurately represent your company, people will come to you expecting a particular experience, and they won't get it.* They will then complain on social media that they didn't get that experience.

If people don't get what they are expecting they can perceive their experience to be negative, even if it is not actually bad.

So if you are told you will get a slice of chocolate cake, and what you are presented with is a smoked salmon and cream cheese bagel, it doesn't mean that what you have been given is bad. You might even like smoked salmon and cream cheese bagels. It's simply that it isn't what you thought you were going to get, and it may not be what you want at that time.

When you are really clear about the narrative, then you will be able to identify opportunities to tell that story, because you know what the story is that you're trying to tell.

Do You Understand The Purpose Of Advertising?

The other key point to understand about social media is that **advertising is also not about instant gratification**. People will often come to Social Media AOK wanting to run ads. They want to know how quickly they can get results, and how many leads they can expect to have generated in the first month.

If you're really looking for solid conversions, then you need to understand the difference between Google advertising and social media advertising.

Google advertising meets an implicit need. You know what you want. You type something into the search bar. You get the results. For example, you're tired, stressed and aching. You'd love a massage. You're also time poor, so you don't want to travel too far. You type in 'Massage. Norwood.'

Social media advertising is implied need. This means that you need to be really clear about who your ideal customer is. Which magazines do they read? What do they like to do at the weekend? Are there particular brands that they like to buy? Do they work in a particular industry, such as retail or fitness?

Once you have worked out who you are targeting, you can put the advert in front of them. If they have an immediate need then it will turn into a lead straight away, where they will follow the call to action.

On the other hand, if they don't have an immediate need, then you create brand awareness. Brand awareness, and brand equity within an audience or a marketplace, is something that builds up over time.

Slow Burn

This is where another common mistake that businesses make comes into play. Companies will try social media for a month or eight weeks. They might even decide to push the boat out and give it a quarter.

What they don't understand is that in those initial three months of using social media, everything is about data driven learning.

During the first month the focus is on figuring out what is and isn't working, split-testing, trying different ads, tweaking campaigns. In the second month you will start to see results, and in the third month you can build on what you have learnt and begin to augment this with additional campaigns.

This means you only really begin to hit your stride in month four. For all the businesses who were in the market for instant gratification, looking for a quick win, they've already turned it off. Because it's not getting the results they want.

Are You Fire Fighting Or Health Checking?

The reasons why people fall into the trap of seeking instant gratification are multi-layered. In a perfect world, you will have road-mapped everything for the next twelve months. You will be working on a twelve-week cycle, so you are looking forward to see where you're going, and looking back to learn from your previous campaigns.

The reality is that most business owners do not plan in this way, and are not that strategic about what they are doing with their social media.

There are good reasons for this. If you are running a small business, then your team might comprise you and three other members of staff. When you go into business, no one explains that one of the most important things you need to do is take a day out at least once a quarter, to health check and plan your goals.

This means that most businesses are lurching from month to month, fire-fighting. At best, they are taking a day every year to work out what they are trying to achieve.

Ideally, you are health-checking things like cash flow and where your new referral opportunities are on a weekly basis. The point at which you integrate your business strategy with your social media strategy is the point at which you become a bit of a powerhouse.

Once everything is aligned and you know why it is that you are doing what you are doing, it becomes much easier to stick to it. *This is because you have a pathway.* You know where you're going, what you're trying to achieve, and the timeframe in which you expect this to happen. You've got all your ducks in a row.

The Golden Rule

I have a golden rule. If it's in the diary, it's in the diary. That means it is non-negotiable. So all of our content planning cycles, our health-checks against our KPIs, all of these things are in the diary. I know exactly when we are sitting down and talking about things and planning things.

Playing the long game isn't just about your social media strategy. It is about every single aspect of your business, because everything feeds everything else.

It's like putting on a stage show. There is a huge amount of planning and rehearsing before you get to opening night. Even when the curtain goes up, there is still a lot going on behind the scenes to ensure everything is running smoothly.

Just because you've got an amazing script, an outstanding cast, and beautiful sets, you don't expect to sell out on the first night. You need to build your audience by consistently putting on a good show, getting great reviews, and building your reputation.

When you reach a point in business where you are defined as successful, people will perceive you as being very lucky. It is never luck. It is hard work, having a plan and a strategy, and taking the time to cement your reputation.

It is a process that takes years. Not many businesses plan years ahead in a way that is actually achievable. Those that do understand that social media is a part of the process.

Where Do You See Yourself In Five Years?

Although I work to a rolling ninety-day plan, I also have a long-term plan. I want to take Social Media AOK to the point where we are the number one agency in Australia for organisation-specific training. Most agencies don't want to take on this role, and so it is quite niche, which makes it more realistic.

So this is my long-term plan. On my ninety-day plan, I have outlined what I need to do during this period to help move us towards fulfilling the long-term plan.

This may include undertaking two interstate speaking engagements in the next twelve weeks, writing at least one thought-leadership post around the importance of humanistic narrative, and reaching out to some of my connections.

It is always good to look and see if it's possible to achieve a couple of your goals at the same time. In this case, my birthday provided me with that opportunity.

Example - Happy Birthday To You?

On the morning of my birthday, I woke up at 7am to find I had 156 'Happy birthday' messages on LinkedIn. I may have had a little bit of a rant.

The reason that I am not a fan of automated reactions on LinkedIn is that all it tells me is that you pushed a button. You have done nothing to further your relationship with me.

In amongst the 156 'Happy birthday' messages, there was one personalised message, from Rex Buckingham at Colour Thinking - a man who has grown his entire business on relationship building.

Rex sent me a lovely message saying he hoped the last year had been a success for me, that he could see I'd taken on a lot of new projects, and he wished me a great year ahead. As well as sending me a lovely birthday greeting, he made it relevant to my business, which was appropriate for the platform.

This gave me the opportunity to write a post saying, '*A HUMANISTIC approach to one- to-one marketing does not mean sending an automated happy birthday message. Please take the time to put some meaning into your correspondence or save us both the time. Congratulations Rex Buckingham for being the only one of my connections out of the 156 who have pushed that button this morning to take the time to personalise the message. Your effort did not go unnoticed and I appreciate you taking the time.*'

Meanwhile, over on Facebook, I got 129 messages from people wishing me a happy birthday. Many of the messages were very similar. Even so, I believe Facebook is a far more appropriate place to send birthday greetings. I also recognised that even if the messages I received were a little generic, I was equally responsible for the relationship. And so I made a decision.

Rather than being irritated by the lack of human connection, I decided to individually respond to each of the people who had wished me happy birthday. I also decided I would ask them something about their lives that connected the dots of the relationship we had.

So this is what I did – and something amazing happened. *Every single person messaged back.* I started conversations with 129 individual people. This meant that I solidified the relationships I had with all 129 of these people – some of whom were business contacts.

It was my birthday. I didn't really have the

spare forty minutes it took me to respond to everyone, but I made the time. This is because the relationships I have with people in my online world are as important as the relationships I have face-to-face, and developing relationships takes time. They are the same relationships - it's just a different mechanism for keeping in touch.

Keep The Noise Down

We've become quite lazy in the digital world. **The thinking should always be to ensure you are not contributing to the white noise.** Whether it is sending out an automated response, posting an inspirational quote superimposed onto a picture of a forest, sharing or liking something that doesn't really support our aims, or creating a piece of content that has little relevance to our audience.

If you really want to be successful in this space, sometimes you have to be prepared to be silent. It's fine to only speak when you have something useful to say. You can ask yourself three simple questions.

Do you have knowledge on a topic? Have you written your post or comment in a way that is going to inspire rather than diminish others? And will it be beneficial to your wider network? If the answer to all three is yes, then by all means share that information.

If you're prepared to talk over others, disregard people's feelings, and rant on any topic regardless of whether or not you actually know what you're talking about, then you may be able to gain attention but the question then becomes, 'What kind of person do you want to be?'

Donald Trump is a perfect example of this type of behaviour. It is all about instant gratification, and it causes a great deal of damage.

The flip side to this, and someone who plays the long game beautifully, is Alexandria Ocasio-Cortez. She is the Twitter queen. Her posts are engaging, informative, interesting and thoughtful.

Once again, it is about what you want to achieve. *If you tie everything back to your own ethics, then you will have a clear idea of how you want to show up in the world.*

This also applies to your business. *What does your business want to be? How do you want people to perceive your company? What do you want to be able to say to yourself about your business?* The really successful companies are going to be asking themselves these questions before they post anything.

They are also going to be thinking about how they answer those questions. For example, people go to Instagram to be inspired. This does not mean you should post endless inspirational quotes. Tell the story of why something is inspiring to you.

Example - Shared Experiences

I have a favourite video that I watch when I need to make a big decision. Last week, I shared this video. I explained that every time I have to take a leap of faith I watch the video to remind myself that it's ok.

I then suggested that anyone in my network who was contemplating a leap of faith might want to check out the video. Context is really powerful. *This is because people then feel that they know you, and that you have shared challenges and experiences.*

It can be hard to build these long-term relationships when you are a company, rather than an individual. This is because it is not as easy for an organisation to make a human connection. It is possible, though.

Example – The Sweetest Taboo

There is a brand new business achieving the human connection beautifully. It is a small company called Taboo. It was started by two young women who were horrified by the lack of access to sanitary products for women and girls in developing countries, and the impact this has on their education and ability to work.

The way they tell their story is all photo driven. They post pictures of the 'Boos' - the Australian girls using Taboo sanitary products.

They take photos of the trucks delivering sanitary products to African schoolgirls.

Every Taboo monthly care package received by an Australian woman provides funding for sanitary products for women in a developing country. So they post photos of the men who have signed their wives and girlfriends up for Taboo products.

There are no lazy, 'just-add-water' motivational quotes. There are photos of empowered people. They are not demanding that you sign up. They are creating a sense of belonging for the women who do.

They are showing their audience what they do and why they do it. They are achieving this by including everyone in the community, and building relationships that will develop over time.

A humanist narrative does not need to be glossy and carefully crafted. It can be as simple and unglamorous as the number of customers you have scrawled across a sanitary towel. *But it is still marketing.*

If I take a snapshot of the chef stuffing a gluten-free hotdog into his mouth then that post will go ballistic. It's not a beautiful photo with an elegant font across it telling people to book a table because we now have gluten-free hotdogs on the menu. It is effective, though, because coeliacs miss hot dogs, and seeing someone enjoying eating one is inspiring. Especially if it's the chef who made it!

In order to be successful in social media we need to make the transition from thinking that marketing is carefully crafted graphics and brilliant branding. It's a big mindset shift for a lot of businesses. We're really good at carefully crafted graphics, and it can feel uncomfortable to step away from that.

A brilliant example of this is the hotel chain that had their customers take photos and use a hashtag with the name of the hotel chain. The hotel then turned the photos into the backs of their room keys, so instead of a generic key it became really personalised.

Do You Know Who Cares About You?

Of course, everybody wants to be able to get that user engagement, and for the bigger companies it is quite easy to do. However, even for the small companies, users will be sharing content about your company. It's just that you probably aren't seeing it. This is where monitoring for mentions of your brand is really useful.

By joining a lot of groups that have relevance to your business, you will begin to see what it is that people are sharing about your company. I am a member of lots of closed Facebook groups for coeliacs.

It always amazes me how many people will post pictures of the food they had at the Duke of Brunswick. If I wasn't a member of the group, then I wouldn't see this content, as it won't come up in search results if it's been posted in a closed group.

Once again, this comes back to being very clear about what it is that you do, and where the people who need your services are going to be. Once you've got an idea about who needs you, the next step is to go out and look for them.

Business dating takes as much time as normal dating. If you want to have great relationships, you can't keep looking for instant gratification. You need to play the long game.

Key Takeaways

- Using social media for business is about cultivating long-term relationships.

- When you're playing the long game, your focus is always on how you can provide value. Think about what you are doing to reach your audience *without selling to them.*

- A humanist narrative does not need to be carefully crafted. The point is to show your audience what you do and why you do it.

Chapter Eight

Measuring Success

Measuring the success of your social media marketing can sometimes feel a little bit like the old question, 'How long is a piece of string?' There are a couple of reasons for this.

Firstly, social media doesn't exist in a bubble - it is always going to be intertwined with all your other efforts. On top of this, although there are elements of your social media that are trackable, there are also many things that can't be tracked.

So what are some of the things that you can easily measure?

Example - Growing The Pie

Back at the Duke of Brunswick, suppose we are aligning our social media to our top-line business goals, and we want to increase our sales from $30,000 a week to $35,000 a week.

In order to achieve this, we've decided to get an extra $1,000 a week in food sales, and we also need to book an extra two functions a week.

Increasing the food sales will happen incrementally. The Duke of Brunswick is a gluten-free pub, so we can work towards this goal by putting some items on the menu that are traditional favourites - things that you can't usually have when you go out for dinner if your diet is gluten-free.

We're coming into winter, and so pies would be a good choice. We can create a range of gluten-free pies that we serve as lunchtime specials. We can then create content around this.

We will be able to measure the success of this content based on whether or not we sell more pies, and also on whether or not our overall lunchtime sales increase.

With the function enquires, we first need to look at how much traffic we currently get to our function page from our social media. We can see this in Google Analytics. We then want to decide what our strategy is for getting more functions.

We might run some Facebook ads aimed at people who are turning fifty or sixty, and who are coeliac or have an interest in gluten-free living.

The ads might say something along the lines of, 'Don't feel like the odd one out on your special birthday.' We're going to send the people who express an interest to a landing page on the website, so we'll be able to see exactly how many enquiries are coming through and how many we're converting.

The Benefits Of Niching

You can see from this that there are some very straightforward ways to measure how successfully you are using social media.

It is worth pointing out that in this example, the people that we targeted in the Facebook ad campaign was a very specific group. The reason for this is that *social media tends to work best when you are talking very directly to a few people.*

Knowing who you are talking to and what you are talking to them about is key. Businesses often get scared of niching to that level, and this can be where you run into trouble.

Example – Trading Places

Let's say you own a car dealership, and you want to talk to anybody interested in buying a Renault. You sell lots of different types of Renault. One of the biggest fleet sales is to trades. Not only do you sell the vans, you also kit them out with everything the tradespeople need and arrange for them to get wrapped with their company signage.

If you could increase your trade sales by 10% then you will reach your sales target. Once you know this, you can then work backwards. If you look at your current rate of enquiry, you can measure how many enquiries you get each month about fleet Renault vans. You can then adjust this seasonally and work out an average over each year or each quarter and start with this number.

If you want to grow this number by 10% you then need to allocate a budget to put behind social media advertising, but also, if this is what you are growing, you can look at what you have already been posting on your social media to promote your fleet sales.

A lot of the time, the answer to this question is going to be stock product images of the vans. It will not be photos of your happy clients in front of their new sign-written vans - even though this would help to build community.

This is because you can tag your clients and then all their mates will see the post, and a proportion of those mates may also be tradies who need new vans.

So now you know who you're talking to, what you want to say to them, and where you can reach them. *This means you can create a much more targeted campaign that is far more likely to give you the results you want.*

It will also be a lot easier to measure. So if you find that your trade sales of fleet vans have increased over the next quarter, you will know your campaign has been successful.

Is Your Traffic Free-Flowing Or Gridlocked?

Outside of this, there are some incidentals that you want to look at. One of these is the volume of traffic that is coming to your website from your different social media channels.

Is one of your goals increasing traffic to your website? If so, have you kept track of what the volume of traffic was for January last year, so that in January this year you can make an educated guess as to whether or not your social media content has helped drive traffic to your website?

It's not rocket science. If the numbers have gone up, then what you are doing is working. If the numbers have gone down then you can look at what you did that broke your traffic flow.

For example, I find that if I haven't been blogging or posting articles on LinkedIn then the volume of traffic from LinkedIn to the website will be down.

Aside from this, you can look at the percentages of traffic to your website, which enables you to measure the number of new visitors as opposed to returning visitors.

You can also put all your conversion tracking in, using Google Tag Manager, to track whether someone has come to your website and completed a transaction.

This transaction doesn't just have to be a sale. It might be that they downloaded something or they submitted a form or they clicked to call. It is also possible to put conversion tracking into your Facebook, LinkedIn and Twitter advertising.

Massaging The Measurements

One problem that a lot of businesses face is that they are held hostage by their agencies. This is because many agencies don't really want to be held accountable.

Rightly or wrongly, there are lots of agencies who will build in loose conversion tracking. This might be that someone who visited your website made it to your contact form, and so they will class this as a conversion – even if the contact form has not been submitted.

It is not uncommon that we pick up clients from other agencies, and they have been told by those agencies that they have a high number of conversions every month, but when you look more closely you see that they are not actually tracking to the end of the transaction.

There is a really simple way to understand how useless it is to measure conversions like this. Imagine you're looking for a date. You go to a nightclub with your mate, and they hand out your phone number to lots of people.

This doesn't mean that you've suddenly got twenty dates lined up. Just because they took your phone number, if no one actually calls you, then you've achieved nothing.

Another problem that businesses run into when they are trying to measure their conversion rates arise with the use of third-party booking engines. If you use a third-party booking engine then there is no capacity to track, because there is no redirect at the end.

What Should You Be Looking For?

It is important to understand what the interim success measures are that you're looking for. Engagement can be one. How many people are actually commenting on your posts? Audience growth can be another. It can be really useful to measure these things, but you do need to distinguish them from actually measuring sales.

It isn't always easy to track back and see how you got to the point of making a sale.

Example - Following The Thread

We work with a number of private hospitals. This came from a referral from somebody that I'd met at a business networking event four years previously. I'd connected to them on LinkedIn, so they had been seeing my content for four years.

They were friends with the general manager of one of the private hospitals, who happened to ask him if he could recommend anyone for social media, because they were getting ready to look at it.

This contract is worth a significant amount of money, and so it certainly equals success. But do I say that this was a social media metric? Do I say that it was a networking metric? *It was both.*

The referral came from someone that I had met at a networking event, but LinkedIn supported me in building that relationship and staying front-of-mind.

Softly, Softly

It can be difficult to measure exactly where your success is routed. *One way that you can measure the more intangible aspects is to look at how cohesive your story is, throughout your organisation across social media.*

There are **soft metrics** that you can use to determine this.

Soft metrics cover all of those things that don't give you a definite box to tick that shows there has been an impact on your bottom line. They cover things like making sure all your customer-facing staff have the same banner image on their LinkedIn profiles, and that the first two paragraphs of their summary talk about what we have improved as a company. These things all join together to show that you are telling a specific story.

Another soft metric is to ensure that all of your content is demonstrating your values as an organisation. You are also measuring this metric when you look at the way you engage with commentary on your accounts.

There are also some **concrete metrics** that you can look at, such as how many ideal clients your sales team has connected with on LinkedIn, and how many of those connections they have turned into coffee meetings.

Mixing It Up

In order to measure your success you should be looking at a mix of soft metrics and concrete metrics. It is important not to abandon the soft metrics, even when your concrete metrics are showing you great results.

The reason for this is that you are looking for cohesion, and it is the soft metrics that will provide you with the information you need about how this is working for you over the long-term.

If you don't understand how to measure your social media success then it can really impact on your business. We worked for eight weeks with a paediatric dental practice. In social media land, eight weeks is a very short period of time.

Example – Leading Themselves Astray

The dental practice who approached us had one big problem. *They believed there was no such thing as soft metrics.* This meant that when I suggested connecting with all the childcare centres in the area, they didn't understand why.

By connecting with the childcare centres, over time they would see the dental practice's content. Once they had established a great online presence in front of the childcare centres, they could then reach out and have a conversation about giving a presentation to the parents or doing something with the kids during oral health week.

Each presentation they gave would put them in front of around fifty families. A percentage of these families may then choose to have that dentist as their family practice. They didn't get it.

What they wanted to do was run lead generation ads targeting mothers in the suburbs surrounding their practice. They wanted 100

> new patients within one month, on a budget
> that really wasn't going to achieve that. It was
> at this point that we all decided they would be
> better off with a different agency.

When you understand that it's a long game, everything else makes sense. You begin to recognise that not all your metrics can be easily measured. You start to see that there is an entire process behind everything you do. You understand that part of this is allocating adequate budgets to your advertising, and part of this is augmenting what your agency does with your own activity.

Basic Mistakes

There is a problem that is even more basic than not understanding what to measure or how. It is also amazingly common. *The problem is not ever looking at your Google Analytics.*

It could be that you don't even have Google Analytics installed on your website. Either way, *it means that you don't know how much traffic is coming to your site from your social media.*

This is something that I see all the time. There are so many companies that have no idea what their average monthly traffic is, how many of those people are new users, what the company's strategy is to drive people to specific content pages and then remarket to those people.

The interesting thing is that many of these companies believe that they are outcomes driven. They are not. If you are truly outcomes driven then you put a really concrete strategy together to get to the outcome.

Often what happens is that they have written several pages for their website that talk about their services. They then post the links to these pages on Facebook. And this is where they stop. They believe they have done everything they need to do in order to get the money flowing in. It doesn't work that way.

Example – Pack It In

If you've ever tried to get a child to pack their lunchbox, then you'll know what I mean. In the process of teaching my children to pack their own lunch we began with conversations about what an adequate lunch looked like.

We had multiple conversations about the difference between a protein source and a carbohydrate source. We spoke about fruit. We spoke about vegetables.

Once we'd had these conversations, we reached the point where they were allowed to make their own sandwiches. After a while they were allowed to pack their whole lunch. Then it got to the point where they were allowed to pack their lunch unsupervised.

The point is that it wasn't an instantaneous process. I didn't wake up one morning and tell my children that they would be packing their own lunch from that day on.

If I had done that, my nine-year-old would

have taken a lunchbox full of Jatz biscuits every day. In fact, he did attempt to do that somewhere in the process, even with all the guidance.

What Are You Doing To Help People?

When it comes to measuring success, you really do need to be keeping an eye on everything all the time. In this way you can make sure you are actually helping people to reach the point that you want them to reach. And if you're not helping them to get there, you can begin to work out why.

It goes back to the understanding that you are using the tool for a purpose. *Social media is there to allow you to be seriously social.* **The seriously component is just as important as the social component.**

Yes, social media can be lots of fun, and it's nice to make friends with lots of people, but you need to take a methodical approach to being social. **You need to tick boxes in a particular order.** *This is because you* *want to build relationships online that mean you can then reach out to people in real life.*

It's a complex ecosystem that you are setting up, and you need to hit all the touch points. Let's go back to the coffee meetings. Imagine you have landed yourself a business date. However, you don't bother exploring what that person is interested or what they care about by looking at the content they are engaging with.

When you go and have that meeting, you may find you have nothing to talk about. **Everything you do is about making it easier for the people you are trying to engage with to engage with you.**

Can You Do It Offline?

Having some structure and some learning around how to engage with people offline can be really helpful with how you approach your activity online.

Joining a BNI chapter is a great way to uncover or sharpen your skills - particularly if you're an introvert. Networking groups such as BNI give you the language, the triggers and the skills to be seriously social in real life, and build on your existing skills. This then allows you to take that model and apply it to social media. And it works.

Moving Beyond The Metrics

As you can see, the way you measure success goes far beyond metrics. You need to look at all the different things you have done each month to improve your business. This will give you a much clearer idea of exactly what it is you have achieved, and the ways in which it has helped.

One of my measures of success is to look at how many people I moved from a place where I barely knew anything about them at all to a place where I knew at least something about them.

I look at how many of my new connections on LinkedIn have gone from just being connections, to having a bit of banter with them online, to catching up for coffee, to finding an opportunity to work together.

As an individual, in terms of success within business, this is what it looks like. From an organisational perspective you need to look at the bottom line and the volume of traffic to the website. However, when it comes to your personal success, it's a different set of measurements entirely.

If you can see that you made achieving your KPIs easier through something that you did online which created an opportunity or made it possible for someone to refer a new client to you, then you have a clear measure of how well you are doing.

Because it is not always a straight line between the two points of action and outcome, it can be much more difficult to understand these ways of measuring your success.

Example - Unexpected Opportunities

I had a phone call this morning from someone from a design agency who had been trying to reach me for a couple of days. I finally had the opportunity to take his call.

We'd had coffee two years previously, and now he was pitching to a client who he felt would really benefit from using social media to tell their story. We spoke about how this could work, and agreed to talk again the following week.

We were connected on LinkedIn, but that was it. I hadn't done anything to maintain the relationship over that two-year period, except put content on LinkedIn.

I didn't know that having that connection was going to turn into a business opportunity, but these things keep happening, and so I know that I am successfully using the platform and doing the things I need to do.

Key Takeaways

- Although success is not always easily measured, if you keep looking at what you are doing online you will develop a clear idea about what is helping you to reach your goals.

- Developing a comprehensive picture of all the ways in which your social media activity is helping you makes it much easier to see where you can be improving your activity.

Chapter Nine

The Definition Of Stupid

So this is the lowdown on all the things people do that they *really* shouldn't do. And there are a lot!

Let's just suppose for a minute that you're a business owner, and you want to use social media to build relationships. However, because you haven't understood exactly how to do this you end up being that party guest who traps someone in the corner and talks about how great they are for hours on end.

The person you are speaking to is valiantly trying to make eye contact with someone else so that they can palm you off onto the other person. Despite their best efforts, it is to no avail. They are still trapped, and you are still talking about yourself. No one wants to be that person.

How Does This Show Up In The Digital World?

In the digital world, this shows up in a couple of different ways. It can be the person who sends every single connection they have on LinkedIn the carefully worded two-page sales email. It can be the person who Facebook Friend requests every single business connection, without really having some common ground.

With social media, it can be very hard to understand where the boundaries lie. In business we spend a lot of time being strategic and having a plan, and being really clear about what we want that plan to achieve for us.

When it comes to social media, we wake up each morning and we dabble. The way we go about this dabbling is dependent on so many external factors. This might be something as basic as not having had enough sleep, or something much more profound, such as what's happening in our business.

For example, if you have urgent cash flow pressures, then it can be easy to hit the 'panic button'. I have seen people throw the same post into ten different Facebook groups, desperately trying to get people to come to their workshop or event, with no individualisation or context.

Fundamentally, the definition of stupid is approaching social media as a broadcast medium, instead of as a human-to-human medium.

You can shift your thinking about every single interaction that you have on social media with one easy trick. Imagine you are sitting across from one other person, telling them a story. It immediately becomes clear what you need to do. **You need to provide entertainment, and you need to provide something of value.**

Distilling your narrative to the point of a single story is quite difficult for many people. Without that single story that articulates who you are, it is very easy to lose your way and get caught up in impulsive content.

Example – Bending Over Backwards

Going back to the trusty old Duke of Brunswick, the story that sums up who we are is simple. We are a seriously social venue. What sits underneath this is that we are the 'bend over backwards' hotel. The reason for this is you have to bend over backwards for people in order to be seriously social. So this is the underpinning premise.

Our job is to recognise what this means in terms of the story. It could be the customer who wants a piece of toast, even though it's not on the menu.

It could be the little girl who gave me a laminated list of all the things she can't come into contact with, and told me she was allergic to life. However it presents itself, we will bend over backwards to provide a seamless, enjoyable, seriously social experience for you.

Between the piece of toast and the little girl who is allergic to life, anything that we put out on our social media, has to fit that story. It may be as a whole new chapter or just an anecdote or even a footnote. Most businesses don't have that measuring stick. They don't have that level of clarity about the difference they make to their customers.

In many cases, businesses define what they do in terms of motherhood statements, broad-brush visions, overarching principles, and values statements. My experience has been that *these things are not executable, because people don't do any work to uncover what it looks like in real life.* They don't know how to live these values or how to demonstrate those lead enterprise behaviours in their businesses.

When you understand that the way you go about demonstrating your vision and values is what creates the stories for your social media marketing, what you do online becomes pretty easy.

What You Give Is What You Get

Once you're aware of exactly what it is that you're giving, you start looking at the world from the point of view of that narrative. You see those snippets of content, you take photos in a different way, you create video in a different way, you engage with your customers and your wider referral partners in a different way.

The reason this happens is that you will see very quickly whether something fits with your narrative or whether it doesn't. You know who your business is, and how your business is in the world.

The other thing that happens is that there is very little tolerance outside of this. And so an incredible side effect is that you have an extremely cohesive brand in real life.

Once you are walking the walk as well as talking the talk, you can then begin to refine what you do. So for the Duke of Brunswick, we have established ourselves as the gluten-free pub, and our chef is looking at what else he can do.

He has decided we don't 'bend over backwards' enough for our vegetarian and vegan customers, and so he is trebling the number of vegetarian and vegan options on the menu.

When you are clear about what you do, you give your teams the opportunity to not only buy into the culture, but to actually develop it.

With the pub, this may be something as simple as noticing that a group of people look a bit squashed around their table, and so we will put together a bigger table and offer it to them, even though they haven't asked us to do this and we are making more work for ourselves.

By taking the trouble to do this, it also means those people are happy for you to take a photo of them having a lovely time and enjoying their meal. *It gives them the opportunity to be anchored and involved in your story.* You're not telling them something, you have made them a part of something. This then makes great content, and so everybody wins.

To paraphrase, stupid can be defined as doing the same thing over and over again, and expecting a different result. Even when we know this, it doesn't stop it from happening.

If You Don't Know Why, How Can Anyone Else?

I ran some training for a group of young people who want to be politicians. They were really struck by the idea that they needed to think about how they were going to tell the story of their party's ethics and values, and how they could tell the 'why' of their movement.

There is a very interesting language that is used in politics, with people being actively encouraged to join a political movement. Why would anyone do this, if all they can see is just another carefully curated candidate?

I want to follow the guy who posts a photo of himself completely drenched, because he's been out door-knocking in the rain. There may well have been a whole bunch of candidates out door knocking in the rain, but who posted the photo showing their commitment to making a difference in their community?

On the other hand, perhaps there was only one who made the effort to go out and brave the storm, and everyone else stayed warm and dry, or sent their junior staff out in their place.

Steve Murray, the liberal MP, does this really well. You'll see photos of him down on his hands and knees changing a tyre while he's on the campaign trail. You'll see photos of him out in the forty-degree heat, red-faced and sweating, meeting and greeting his constituents. It might not be pretty or glamorous, but it's real life, and what we are always trying to do on social media is connect with people in real life.

Bridging The Gap Between Online And Offline

The younger generation is definitely driving a shift away from the gloss and glamour of the past. They have grown up on social media, and so there is far less separation for them between their lives online and their lives offline.

The advent of the stories format, which is much more raw, and authentic, and unedited, has built demand for brands to follow suit. There is an expectation of transparency.

This means that **the successful businesses will**

be the ones that are comfortable being raw, and comfortable *telling a story*, rather than *selling a story*. Anyone can get out there and try to sell a story, but that doesn't mean people are going to want to buy it. When you tell a story, everybody engages.

So how do you begin to make that switch?

The first step is to choose your platforms wisely. The 'stories' format allows companies to get comfortable with the idea of telling, rather than selling. The 'stories' format is ephemeral, disappearing within twenty-four hours of being posted.

This means that people can be less concerned that the content they create is still going to be sitting online next week, and so they can test things and try things in a way that is less scary.

Beyond that, with content that is a little more permanent, it is about just dipping your toe in the water and reassuring yourself that you're going to be ok.

It's Not About The Money

Start by articulating really clearly and succinctly who you are, either as an individual businessperson or as an organisation, in a way that reveals what motivates you beyond money – so what your 'why without a dollar sign' is.

Find a story that you can tell about one customer to illustrate that 'why', in a way that allows anyone to understand it. Once you have done this, you can then begin to look at how you can create more of those stories.

The next stage is developing cohesion throughout your organisation, so that everyone is taking the same approach. People can see things and interpret things very differently, so this can often take time and effort, even when you are leading by example. It can be painful to get cohesion. You can't just drag everyone along kicking and screaming.

As Patrick Lencioni says, you can't over-communicate the vision. You want to be clear about your vision, and communicate it again and again. You want to ask your team every day how the things they are doing fit with who the business is. For my businesses, this means asking how people have been authentic, flexible, and fluid. In essence, how they were seriously social.

Listen To Your People

Once you have asked this question, you reach the most important point. *You then need to shut up and listen.* If you find that there is a disparity between what you are trying to achieve and what they are doing, there are a number of exercises that you can do.

For example, you can talk about brand pillars, to solidify what the company stands for, so are you an emotive brand or a discovery brand, and so on. Often, though, the first step is to find out why people choose to work within your business.

This will offer some insight into what is important to them. You can then ask what they love about working within the company – the things they would hate to see change.

When you come to people from this perspective, so that you listen first, and find out what people think before you offer your opinions, then you will have a much better idea of what is actually going on.

When you are the leader, if you tell people your thoughts before asking them for theirs, you will almost certainly find that no one will offer a different view or opinion to yours.

Even in marketing, we have to get better at asking questions and then being quiet for a little bit, to see what comes. The beauty of this is that when you encourage your teams to have really robust conversations about who you are, how you can demonstrate that, and how to tell that story online, they have way better ideas than you.

Your only job from there is to finesse the execution of the ideas. And the magic is that you have buy-in. After all, it wasn't *your* idea, it was *their* idea.

You can then set aside time to health check this once a quarter. You can have a group conversation with whoever is responsible for steering the marketing ship, and find out how you are going with telling the story of who you are and what you're about.

More than this, you can ask who has ideas for how to tell the story the following month. When you take this approach, it is a very different lens to, 'have we done the posts about the 20% off sale?'

Are You Riding The Waves Or Rolling Into Shore?

Relationship based content is so much more rewarding for your teams and your customers than transactional content. When you shift the focus from what your business does to why your business does those things, people want to be part of the why.

The new wave of businesses coming through has a far more natural understanding of how to do this. So for existing businesses, the choice really is to learn how to surf or gently roll into shore.

This younger generation has parents who are highly educated, highly articulate, and who have often done a lot of personal and professional development work.

As a result, the generation that has come up behind them has picked up the ball and run with it. They are highly articulate and extremely well-informed about the world they live in. *The key difference is that they are not afraid of being seen in the way that the Generation Xers are.*

If you come from the generation that was taught not to try and stand out from the crowd, how do you overcome that fear and tap into what the younger generation are naturally doing?

You need to build up a bank of empirical evidence that shows you the sky is not going to cave in. Make a little decision, throw it out there, reassure yourself that nothing bad happened, and then throw it a little further out the next time.

Keep Yourself In The Driving Seat

If you have younger members of your team, even though the temptation can be to give them the keys to your social media, *that is not the answer!* It's like giving them the keys to your Maserati and hoping for the best.

What you can do, though, is allow them to be your navigator. Keep yourself in the driving seat, but listen to where it is they suggest you go. Smart people take advice from everywhere. What you choose to do with that advice is up to you.

Sometimes we ignore the GPS – even if that is at our peril. Sometimes the GPS may have got it wrong, and be trying to drive us over a cliff. You need to have some discernment, but don't be afraid to let someone else in the car with you.

If you do decide that you want to have a navigator, you still need to set the parameters. Tell them where you're going, and then ask how they propose you get there. At this point, you need to have a really robust discussion about the route they are suggesting, to see if it is going to be the best way forward. This is how you start to see different ideas.

Don't Be Afraid To Ask For Outside Help

Having a consultant who specialises in a humanistic approach to social media marketing can be really beneficial. These consultants can be very hard to come by. This is because marketers are taught to sell things, and to foster brand demand and product demand.

As a result, marketers have lost the art of storytelling. Having said this, there are a number of social media marketing companies out there, mine included, who are really focused on storytelling. So even if it takes a little time and effort, it is possible to find someone who can help you to achieve your aims.

Seeing The Macro And The Micro

You can think of the process as a hermeneutic circle, where your understanding of the whole story you are telling is dependent on your understanding of each part of the story, and vice versa.

You need to focus on the bigger picture, and also on the individual pieces of the puzzle. *If you only see in macro or micro then you lose the sense of what you are doing.*

If you become too concerned about getting it wrong or being seen in a specific way then the whole thing falls apart. With time and practice, you can learn to relax into what you are doing and trust.

Ultimately, you just need to try things and see what happens. If you get negative feedback, you can deal with it without personalising it. Sometimes negative feedback can be constructive.

Learn To Trust Yourself

If you are very unsure about your content it may be helpful to run things by your team or your referral partners before you launch anything out into the world.

Equally, it is important to realise that each of these people will have their own views and opinions, and you will almost certainly never get it exactly right in everyone's eyes.

Example – Lipstick, Powder And Paint

A few years ago, when video was just about to explode, I signed up for a thirty-day course to learn about creating online video content. You had to make a video every day for thirty days, which was great. However, the course was delivered by a former TV presenter, and this person had a very clear view of how things should be done.

Their view was that women should always wear makeup on camera. Particularly lipstick. They were also of the opinion that it was essential to wear bright, eye-catching colours.

Now, anyone who has ever met me knows that I'm not much on makeup. At best, I might put some mascara on if I'm feeling a little tired. However, I was paying an expert to guide me, and so I followed the rules. I put on my eye makeup and my bright red lipstick. Even though I usually wear blacks and greys I put on an electric blue dress. And I made my video.

The moment I put my video up online the messages started pouring in. 'What in God's name is that?' 'What is on your face?' 'What are you wearing?' 'When did you get your ears pierced?' It quickly became abundantly clear that I wasn't being authentic to who I was. I was doing what someone else thought I should do.

My response to all the feedback was to ask if people had listened to what I was saying. The response was universally the same – they had all

> been too busy staring at the person on screen, and they had no idea what I had been talking about.

Sifting Through The Feedback

People have their own agendas. Different personality styles take in information in different ways. This means that if you ask a high 'D' and a high 'I' for feedback, they will be likely to pick up on different things.

It's good to get feedback, but you need to take all the feedback, and then go back and see if it sits with who you are, or if it belongs to the other person. You can then work out which bits to ignore, and which bits are useful.

It can be difficult. For example, high 'D' personalities tend to take feedback with a grain of salt. They tend to assume they know best. This means if you are a high 'D' then you have to actively cultivate the capacity to take in feedback.

'C' type personalities can obsess over that

feedback, and find a whole heap of articles to explain why the feedback is or isn't valid. The 'S' type personality will just curl up in a foetal position for a little while, until they have reconciled themselves to the fact that someone was unkind to them.

Even though it can be tough for generation Xers to feel comfortable being seen, the one advantage is that something magical happens once you pass the age of forty. You begin to edit yourself less.

This is a really strong standpoint to be working from, because when you are looking at someone who is really in touch with who they are and what their narrative is, the effect is powerful.

Key Takeaways

• By shifting your thinking about how to interact
online, you gain clarity about what you need
to do. In every interaction, you need to provide
entertainment and value.

• Learn to trust that it is ok to be seen. By taking
small steps every day, you will soon find you have
made great progress.

• Keep yourself in the driving seat. It can be helpful
to ask for directions from those around you, but you
still need to choose the destination.

Chapter Ten

Staying Relationship Focussed

To ensure you are staying relationship focussed you need to understand one thing. *You don't know the ripples you are creating with your online activity.* Social media is fantastic, if you remember that every single person is a potential customer or a potential referral partner.

A Little Knowledge Can Be A Dangerous Thing

Think of it like this – there are ten of us sitting round a dinner table. We have never met each other before. We're all introduced, but the only information we get is everyone's name and job title. We don't know what industry anyone is in, we don't know their backstory, we don't know where they went to school, or what their hobbies and interests are.

We have to make some judgements about what we say and what we do. And we need to make sure we get it right. Because other than the names and job titles of the dinner guests, we have been told that one person at the table has a contract that can change the face of our business forever. *This is essentially what social media is!*

There will be a handful of individuals in the ocean of hundreds and thousands of people who probably, at some time, will have a requirement for your services, or will be your introduction to many introductions.

This means that it is *always* so important that you're not rude, abrupt or flippant to anyone. You need to take time to frame what you say in a way that is going to be palatable to most human beings.

Where Are You Putting Your Focus?

The divide between palatable and fake can be very narrow. As a result, you can find yourself treading a very fine line. This comes back to the 'Happy birthday' saga. Because I take a humanistic approach to social media, I responded personally to every single birthday greeting that I received. *With a relatable piece of information that was relevant to that person.*

The focus is always on kindness and adding value. Let's look at a real world example here. Most of us know someone who takes twenty minutes to get to the point. In this instance, the kind thing to do is ask if it would be ok to give them some feedback. Let them know it could help make them more money or give them a better return on their time investment. *Asking permission is key.*

If the answer is yes, then you can be both honest and kind when you give the feedback. You can also acknowledge your own shortcomings as part of that honesty. So I know that one of my failings is that I am not good with minutia.

This means I can explain to the person that one of my faults is that I tune out if I'm given too much detail. I can let them know that as a result of this, when they started talking to me about how many DPI were in a blah blah blah, they lost me at 'DPI'.

Online, exactly the same things apply. You take the time to be kind and add value, because the relationship is the most important thing. One way you can achieve this is by always responding to people's queries.

How many LinkedIn messages do you get that you never respond to? Social media is about building relationships, so even if you receive an unsolicited LinkedIn message, it is always worth taking the time to reply.

Checking Every Link

If somebody sends me an unsolicited LinkedIn message about a business opportunity, I always respond. I will say I can see they are very excited about this new multi-level marketing product, and they clearly enjoy their involvement.

I will then explain that my capacity for additional side projects is currently at zero, but I appreciate them taking the time to reach out to me. This is significantly kinder and more helpful than either ignoring them completely or sending a terse message that essentially tells them to get stuffed.

Multi-level marketers are educated to seek out

people with healthy networks, and so if you fall into this category you are very likely to receive these kinds of messages. And they can be annoying. *But what happens if the person who is really excited about the multi-level marketing opportunity is related to the CEO of the company you really want to get into?*

In every single exchange the questions need to be, **'Have I enriched the relationship with this person or not?'** and **'Have I taken the opportunity today to build somebody up online?'**

Example – Taking The Time To Make A Difference

How you enrich your relationships may well be different every time. For example, Matt from iElectrical recently took time out of his day to come to the hotel and take a photo of something and craft an email to keep one of my clients happy.

As a result, I took a happy snap of Matt in his shirt with the company logo, and wrote a Facebook post. I let people know that the fact he'd gone out of his way for me was one of the reasons I love his company. It was a last minute request, but nothing is ever too hard for iElectrical, and you can't ask for a better company than that.

Yes, it took thirty seconds of my time, but that's all it took. Is Matt going to take the opportunity to help me when he can? Yes. Did I enrich the relationship? Yes. Would it have detracted from the relationship if I'd done nothing? No, but I wouldn't have strengthened it at all.

It's not necessarily that the ties don't already exist within the relationship. It's just that if you keep on adding to them then the connection gets stronger and stronger. When you have created enough ties then you have a relationship that can really support your business in a fantastic way. It's the difference between having one strand of cotton and a beautifully woven rope.

Banking On Your Future Success

Social media is a great way to put money in the relationship bank for when you need it. If you're proactively looking for ways to strengthen your relationships and add value to your connections, then when you need a favour, you have enough money in the bank to make a withdrawal. This doesn't mean that you can make withdrawals all the time. You need to put in more than you take out, to maintain a healthy balance.

There is a common mistake that people make which illustrates this point. It looks like this: Fred is connected to Peter and Jane on LinkedIn. Peter would really like to be connected to Jane. Peter makes Fred feel as though he has a responsibility to make the introduction. The problem is that nobody feels good about the guy who only ever gets in touch when they want something.

If someone else has a nice big juicy network, it doesn't mean you get to turn up to the table with an empty plate and ask for a slice. **If you want people to share, then you need to make a contribution.** You can't expect other people to foot the whole bill, and certainly not on a first date.

Are You Hunting Or Farming?

There is a challenge with looking at things from the perspective of what you can get rather than what you can give. *When you are constantly hunting instead of farming you never actually grow anything.* This means that you continually have to move to new hunting grounds, because you quickly exhaust the supply of food in one area.

If you're farming, this means that you're looking for ways to give, by nurturing and building your networks. This might be through giving recommendations on LinkedIn, reaching out, sharing good content, or connecting people to other people for mutual benefit.

When you take this approach, something wonderful happens. *You don't have to leave your house.* This is because you have built an amazing garden that solves all of your problems.

The tenet of being seriously social is that it is not just an online thing. It's a way of being in business that works online and offline, and capitalises on both in a way that is genuine and authentic. Even if there is an awareness that you may benefit from the relationships that you cultivate, that is not even truly what lies at the heart of it.

When you make human connections there is an automatic return on that investment, because you feel like a good person. And when you feel like a good person then your life is a little bit more fun.

If you've ever met someone who is really materialistic and driven by what they can get out of other people, they have a certain energy about them that isn't attractive to be around.

Is Your Social Media Activity Making A Difference To Anyone?

Social media is a fantastic tool to build a community. It's a great place to share stories and resources, and to create interconnected networks. When you approach it with this relationship-based focus, rather than being content based, it happens very organically. Once again, this is about storytelling instead of 'storyselling'.

To tell a story you have to create the moments that go into weaving the narrative. This is really what keeping relationship focussed is about. You are creating those moments. Essentially, it is another example of the difference between being efficient and being effective.

Efficiency could be connecting to 10,000 people. The problem is that if you don't have a relationship with any of these people, having those connections it is not particularly effective.

To be effective, you could start off by connecting with 500 people. You engage with their content. You take time to find out about what is important to them. You volunteer some insights that are aligned with the challenges they are facing. You connect them to somebody who does what they need help with, so they can have a conversation.

So how do you achieve all of this, without it distracting you from everything else you need to do?

It's very simple. Even if you have a network of thousands, *you only give this level of attention to a small number of people.* **Aim to make a difference to three**

people every day. That's all, and that's achievable for anyone.

Let's say you've got fifteen LinkedIn messages that you need to respond to. Some of these messages will be three word answers, and to some you can copy and paste a message requesting that the person calls your office to book a meeting.

This may leave three messages that you need to give your full attention to. By spending five to ten minutes writing responses to these messages, you will have achieved your goal.

Are You Setting Realistic Expectations?

Setting expectations is important, for you and for others. Sometimes someone will message a booking request for the pub through private messaging on a Saturday, when I'm not at work. However, I appreciate that hotels are open seven days a week, so I will often respond to them – *but I won't try to fix their problem*.

Let's say they want to make a booking. I can't see what the availability is because I'm not at the pub. If

I try to take the booking, I'll only make things more complicated for everyone. If I double booked a table this would lead to a bad experience for the customer, and would create headaches for my staff.

I will let the person know that I'm at home with my kids, and that I will be back at work the following day. I do this, because it lets them know I'm a human being. They are still getting a response, but I'm not trying to fix the problem when I'm not actually in a position to help.

Even when you're bending over backwards, it needs to be in a way that is realistic and sustainable. You can't always be trying to fix the problem and solve everything for everyone. We've all met that person, and they are both exhausted and exhausting. They are stressed, tired and wired. And through trying to please all the people all the time, they inevitably end up letting some of those people down.

No one requires you to be that person. You can set the parameters and be honest. We get taught not to be honest from a very young age, from the point when we're told not to be silly or not to cry. The message is that what we think, and particularly what we feel, isn't valuable or wanted. Finding your way through this can be tough.

Creating Hierarchical Relationships

By breaking things down into manageable pieces, the feeling that you need to be all things to all people quickly dissolves. An easy way to do this is by understanding that in business, your relationships are hierarchical. You have a top three, a top ten, and then there's everybody else.

Prioritise the people in your top three. If they text or message, always respond within the hour. If they call, unless you're in a meeting, answer the phone even if you're doing something else. **With the people ranked from four to ten, ensure you respond to their messages or calls the same day.**

The minute someone is out of the top ten, then the level of priority shifts. It is still important that you respond to people in a reasonable timeframe, but you can give yourself more leeway, and select a time that is more convenient to you.

When you are focussing on building really solid relationships it is crucial to get really clear about which people in your social media landscape are in your top three and your top ten. It matters, because these people are the ones you need to be reaching out to and having conversations with.

We all have somebody in our network who does this stuff really well. Because they understand how to prioritise, it means that they create space to meet everyone's needs. They respond to every email. They send follow up notes. They let you know the value you have given them, and they express appreciation for what you do.

It doesn't matter how high up the ladder someone has climbed. You will find people right at the top of their professions who still behave in this way, and the respect they command is enormous.

Extending A Helping Hand

A business associate of mine contacted me last week to say that his daughter was doing some research for a LinkedIn project. Last week I was ridiculously busy. However, I was

happy to answer the questions in her survey, even though they demanded a certain level of detail.

I took the time to answer the questions because it was the right thing to do. Yes, there is a chance that one day she may end up working somewhere that opens doors for me, but that's not really the point. It's important to understand and recognise that if you are in a position to give, then that it is a good thing to do.

For example, I got a LinkedIn message from a migrant last week. He was really experienced marketing internationally, but he had no contacts here. I put him in touch with a few people who could help him. I didn't have to do that, but it cost me nothing to help him except a little bit of time.

This brings us to the next point, which is that *people who are good at relationships are usually programmed to help.* Every time I answer the phone, the first words I say are, 'How can I help?' It works, because it automatically gets you into the frame of mind where you're thinking about what you can do for that person. It also focuses them on the reason why they called, so you cut out all the waffle.

Being helpful doesn't have to be time consuming. It doesn't have to take up your whole day. At first, having a relationship-based focus may feel constructed and clunky, because it's not how we're taught to live in the world. Generally speaking, at school and in business, we're taught to be very transactional.

This means that in the beginning it can feel like a headache. You're not sure how to do it or how to make the pieces fit. But the more you do it, the more natural it becomes. This continues, until you get to a point where it is an automatic way of being, and digital just becomes one part of that. Once you reach this point, it becomes effortless. And when it becomes effortless, you begin to get the real returns.

Key Takeaways

• Remember that the relationship is always the most important thing.

• Take the time to frame what you say in a way that is going to be palatable to most people.

• When you keep adding to your existing ties then the connection gets stronger and stronger.

• Aim to make a difference to three people every day.

• Help when and where you can, but ensure it's realistic and sustainable. You don't have to solve everything for everyone!

Conclusion

Checklist For Success

When it comes down to making the most of your newfound knowledge about how to be a human being online, which is really all that we've been talking about, it helps to have a plan of execution. In order to be effective, it's important to put things into place in an ordered and methodical way.

Here is a ten-step check list to ensure you are on track with your social media.

Step One – What Is The Story You Are Telling?

You can start with the premise that the very first thing that you need to do is to distil who you are, either as a business or as a person, into a single story that demonstrates the truth of who you are. Let's be honest – this is a big ask for anybody. However, you can't do anything else until you've figured that bit out. *You need to have the story in order to create the narrative, because it will help guide you as you go.*

Step Two – How Are You Going To Tell Your Story?

Once you have the story, you need to think about what you do in real life that tells similar stories. What are the other pieces of the puzzle that your customers encounter? And how do you win the hearts of your customers before you win the sale? In thinking about this, you will start to gather some ideas around your content.

Step Three – Have You Planned Ahead?

From here, you can move to the giant calendar on the wall. Have you planned out what happens during the year, and how you're going to make the most of that? This is about ensuring you understand the ebbs and flows of your business, and what's important. Have you looked at what your business goals are, how social media is meant to support them, and how being seriously social in real life is going to back that up?

Alongside this planning, there are several other questions you need to ask yourself. Have you formulated exactly what a connection strategy looks like to you? Do you clearly understand how you create value, and what that value looks like? Have you thought about how much of your content you're going to put money behind?

You don't need to have a perfect plan for the entire year. However, you can map all of these things out so that you have a clear twelve-week plan. Once this is done you can then start looking at what's working and what isn't, and refining this, then you can't help but get better.

Step Four – Are You Dressed For Success?

After you have done your planning, the next step is to ensure you have the right outfit. If I were to go and look at your social media channels or your business profiles - or the business profiles of any of the people working in your company – would they represent you well? Do they all feature the same banner image? Does this image convey your story? Are your profile pictures congruent with who you are as a company?

Example – Positive Impression

How you tell this story and what this congruence looks like may not always be as straightforward as ensuring you've got your best suit on. A great example of this is a Facebook Live video that Scott Morrison recently put out.

He had clearly been very well instructed. He wasn't wearing what I would have expected from the leader of the Liberal Party, which would be a grey suit with a blue tie. He wasn't standing on a podium in front of the Australian flag. He was sitting on a couch, leaning forward, with his shirt sleeves rolled up. His shirt was a pale yellow, with the top button undone, and there was no tie. He was talking quietly, and looking directly into the camera.

Because none of this was what I expected from the prime minister, I watched for longer than I normally would have. This was because he was connecting with me in a way that I hadn't anticipated. He was communicating with me in a way that was very frank and open, and it unpacked a lot of the narratives I had about him in the space of two and a half minutes. I was impressed.

Why it worked so well is that he was dressed for the story he was telling. The video went out at eight o' clock on a weeknight. It went out on Facebook, not the evening television news. The language was straightforward, with a lot of real life examples that the audience could relate to. *All of this goes back to understanding how you position yourself in the digital community.*

Step Five – Are You Giving Yourself Enough Time?

As you can see, each step in the checklist requires a methodical approach. The reality is that **whenever you're learning a new skill, you have to start off by being methodical.**

My approach to social media these days is very organic. From the outside looking in it may seem quite haphazard. But it works. This is because I spent a long time being very methodical and learning my craft, and getting better at telling the story. Eventually I stopped caring if I was telling a story or not, and just got on with the business of being a human.

It's like learning to dance. You have to learn the steps. You have to move from conscious incompetence to unconscious competence. It takes time. *So how long does this take?* To an extent, it depends how big your teams are and what your role is.

Let's say that you're a sales person, and you make the shift to social selling. When you first start, it might take you four hours a week in a single block to plan out all your content. You may then have to spend thirty minutes a day to get everything onto the platforms and engage with your audience. The reason for this is that you're still learning how to use all the tools, and you're still finessing your story.

Once you know what you are doing, and you are confident that everything is unfolding as you intended, it's probably still going to take two hours a week in a single block, and five to ten minutes twice a day outside of that, if you're going to do your social media well.

Example – Flower Power

A great example of someone who does their social media really well comes from another social media provider. I had been invited to give an Instagram masterclass, and while I can teach it, it's not my core purpose. As a result, I put Rubina Carlson forward.

Rubina is the digital marketing manager for Sealink Travel Group, and she is particularly passionate about Instagram. Not only this, but she has also been teaching social media courses at TAFE for a long time. I know all of these things about her because we're connected on social media.

She was very excited to be giving a masterclass on her favourite subject to two hundred delegates from the hospitality industry. In fact, she was so excited that, on the morning of the conference, the most enormous bunch of flowers arrived for me.

At first I thought that my partner Alex had

sent me 'just because' flowers, as he sometimes does. I was all warm and glowing, and then when I saw the card nestled amongst the flowers that glow became even warmer. Although I love getting flowers from my partner, to be acknowledged in this way by Rubina was even more special – because it was totally unexpected and extremely thoughtful.

The note said that she really appreciated that I had put her name forward to speak at the conference, and that she hoped I had a fantastic day. The first thing I did was to take a photo of the flowers, and tagged her all over social media, thanking her for her kindness. This is a great example of being human, and melding the two worlds.

She didn't need to send me flowers, and I didn't need to post a photo of them. Because she understands how it all works, she didn't take a picture of herself with the flowers, and write a post to say how she's bought them for Simone Douglas at Social Media AOK as a thank you for recommending her as a speaker.

This would be an example of exactly how not to do it.

Step Six – Are You Regularly Checking In With Everyone?

One point that is worth looking at a little more deeply is how you monitor the personal accounts of your teams. First and foremost, this is where it becomes really important to hire for cultural fit. If people can't demonstrate your core values at interview, then they can't play.

There is nobody on my team who doesn't understand being seriously social as a way of life. As a result of this, they can adapt how they behave across social media to fit with their work environment. This means you can give them a little bit of license.

If this is not the case, you still don't get to dictate how the people on your teams use social media – in or out of work. *If you try and do this, you will not get buy in.* So instead of telling people what they have to post on which day or what they may not do on their personal accounts, you need to take a different approach.

Have a round table discussion about what opportunities are available to really get the company's message out. Ask how you can all use your digital presence, both personally and professionally, to improve the business and reach more customers. Find out what people are comfortable with and what ideas they have. *And then shut up and listen for a while.*

If you've got a really poor culture in your workplace this still won't work. If this is the case, then before reading this book you should really be reading a book about how to improve your business culture. **You can't implement peak values around humanist marketing and narratives if your culture doesn't support it.** It just won't happen.

When you have a great culture, you need to consistently come back to your team and ask if anyone has any ideas, and offer up your own suggestions for people to discuss. Sometimes I think I've had a great idea, and someone else will say it goes too far. You really do need to keep talking to your teams, as well as checking in with yourself.

If you do not do this, there is a danger of hubris. It's all very well to think you know what you're doing and saying, but it could be that you're getting too big for your boots. If this is the case, things are going to get uncomfortable for you pretty quickly. So **you need to consistently seek feedback.** You don't have to be everyone's cup of tea. You do need to make sure you are your ideal customer's cup of tea.

This means that, **as well as checking in with yourself and your teams, you also need to be checking in with your ideal customers.** A great way to do this is through email newsletters. Not the monthly 'selling at the customers' newsletter. *This is about sending a personalised email to your customers.*

Imagine you send a message that says, 'Hey Ted, I wrote a couple of blogs last month. I'm not really sure if they cover what is of interest to your industry at the moment. Would you mind having a quick look, and if there is another topic that you'd like to see, could you flick me a quick email, as I'm looking for content ideas.'

So Ted gets a plain text, non-branded email from Simone. If you send a plain text email from Mail Chimp it looks like it came from your personal account. It doesn't need a header. It doesn't need a whole heap of branding all over the place. If they are an existing customer, then they've seen your branding before. **What your existing customers have that is valuable to you is the knowledge about how you can help them.**

Not only this, they will also really value being asked, because everybody likes to have their opinion heard. This means that it becomes another way to win over a customer. We live in a very busy society, and people are often not asked for their opinion. Essentially, by asking what they think, they do the work for you.

This is why social media is not as hard as people think. Yes, it takes some time to set it all up. Yes, it takes some time to get the structure in place and learn **what to ask, when to ask,** and **how to ask it.** Notice that I'm using the word 'ask' a lot here. It's not what to tell, when to tell, and how to tell it. *The people that you're talking to would like to have a conversation with you.* It's up to you to give them that opportunity.

When you're really busy, it isn't always easy to stay in a place where you are very relationship focussed. For a few months after I took over the pub, I really didn't pay attention to what was happening with Social Media AOK.

Once I finally found my equilibrium again, I realised there was something missing. It was our humanist narrative. I had assumed that everybody else lived in my head and knew that I didn't just want them posting a whole heap of statistics.

If I had consistently checked in with everybody, and asked what stories we had, and if there were any customers we needed to have conversations with, then everything would have stayed on course. No matter how busy you are, you always need to ensure you're steering. Otherwise, you can very quickly go off track.

It goes back to the point that you don't give the keys to the car to anyone else. If it is appropriate and they have the skills, you can let them navigate. However, you always need to keep yourself in the driving seat.

Step Seven – Are You Evolving?

Something else to be aware of is that you need
to be prepared to evolve. As the platforms evolve
and different opportunities present themselves,
be prepared to spend some time getting your head
around whether or not these things fit with what you
want to achieve.

Step Eight – Can You Say 'No'?

It is also worth remembering that it's ok to say
'no'. It's ok to decide that certain platforms don't
work for you. You don't need to be on every single
platform. And with the platforms that do work
for your business, it's ok not to use every possible
function just because it's there.

Example – Filtering Out The Nonsense

I was recently running a Facebook Live training
session, and I started messing around with
augmented reality filters. For the next twenty-
four hours, my Facebook page featured a video
of me giving a short speech about how to go

live to a Facebook page, with a moustache and turban. This is something I'd never have said in a pink fit that you would see me doing in public.

However, in order to make the class more engaging, I thought I might as well. I then had a conversation with them, saying that, while I recognised it was vastly entertaining for them, the reality was that I never wanted to see an accountant or a financial advisor on Facebook with a cartoon moustache and turban. Maybe if you're a comedian or talking to young people then these kinds of filters may be appropriate, but it really does need to fit with your story.

Step Nine – Are You Able To Let Go?

Don't be afraid to deactivate accounts. Let's say you have been using something as part of your digital strategy. After some time, you come to a point where it no longer fits with your strategy. Don't leave it sitting in space, inactive. Delete it. Deactivate it. Unpublish it. If I go to that account and it hasn't been used for months, my assumption is likely to be that the business is closed.

Step Ten – Check, Check, And Check Again!

Keep asking yourself the three key questions. Does your activity align with what you are trying to achieve? Are you clear about who you are trying to be? Do you know what you want your customers to feel? If you can answer 'yes' to all of these questions, then it means there is intelligence behind your content. And this means you can feel confident that you are being seriously social.